The Climax of Biblical Prophecy

A Guide to Interpreting Revelation

I0809521

Also in the Biblical Discernment for Difficult Issues Series:

The Law and the Christian: God's Light within God's Limits
Love, Liberty, and the Christian Conscience: Striking the Biblical Balance
Upright Downtime: Making Wise Choices about Entertainment
The Glory Due His Name: What God Says about Worship
Handling Earthly Treasure: Biblical Certainties about Money
Love Not the World: Winning the War against Worldliness

The Climax of Biblical Prophecy

A Guide to Interpreting Revelation

Brian Hand

JOURNEYFORTH
ACADEMIC

GREENVILLE, SOUTH CAROLINA

Library of Congress Cataloging-in-Publication Data

Hand, Brian R., 1975-
The climax of biblical prophecy : a guide to interpreting Revelation / Brian R. Hand.
p. cm.
Summary: "A guide to answering crucial interpretive questions in Revelation"—Provided by publisher.
Includes bibliographical references.
ISBN 978-1-60682-388-0 (perfect bound pbk. : alk. paper)
1. Bible. N.T. Revelation—Criticism, interpretation, etc. I. Title.
BS2825.52.H35 2012
228'.06—dc23

2012007875

BWHEBB [Hebrew] and BWGRKL [Greek] Postscript® Type 1 and TrueTypeT fonts Copyright © 1994–2006 BibleWorks, LLC. All rights reserved. These Biblical Greek and Hebrew fonts are used with permission and are from BibleWorks, software for Biblical exegesis and research.

The fact that materials produced by other publishers may be referred to in this volume does not constitute an endorsement of the content or theological position of materials produced by such publishers.

All Scripture is quoted from the Authorized King James Version unless otherwise noted.

The Climax of Biblical Prophecy: A Guide to Interpreting Revelation
Brian Hand, PhD

Design and page layout by Michael Boone

© 2012 BJU Press
Greenville, South Carolina 29614
JourneyForth Academic is a division of BJU Press.

Printed in the United States of America
All rights reserved

ISBN 978-1-60682-388-0

15 14 13 12 11 10 9 8 7 6 5 4 3 2

For Elisabeth—
May He come in your days,
putting an end to evil,
establishing His kingdom,
filling the earth with His glory.

Contents

Introduction

Just before we went to our first laboratory class in college chemistry our teacher called for our attention. "You must be very careful to follow the instructions," he intoned. "Just give us the chemicals," we countered in our own thoughts. He continued after a brief pause, "These chemicals can be extremely hazardous. Don't make mistakes. A few years ago I checked on a student just before she mixed two chemicals together. As she started to pour one into the other, I snatched the beaker out of her hand. Had she combined those chemicals, she would have blown up the lab and injured or killed herself and the other students in the room." Suddenly, all rustling stopped. Every eye followed the instructor. Our faces were grave. We realized, probably for the first time, that failure to know and apply the rules of chemistry has serious consequences.

Chemistry provides an apt analogy to our study of Revelation because both have a dizzying array of possibilities and procedures for their proper use. Not all possibilities are good. Some are dangerous. A misinterpretation of Revelation will not "destroy the lab," but it will obscure the Author's meaning and intent, leaving the reader with a weakened or misdirected outcome.

Revelation is an unusual book, but it is hardly impenetrable. The fact that many interpreters have used it as a happy hunting ground for their imaginations does not diminish its value for us. We may find Revelation more difficult to grasp than many other books of Scripture, but some commentators magnify its difficulty unnecessarily.

We don't need to wonder whether to take Matthew's Gospel figuratively or literally. We don't wonder whether the book of Exodus is futurist, idealist, historicist, or preterist.[1] We don't have to consider whether Proverbs is practically applicable to life or just historical information. But all of these questions come to bear on our interpreting Revelation.

Instead of scaring us away from the text, these questions should drive us to it. God gave this book to His church. We can understand Revelation adequately if we are willing to follow proper procedures of interpretation. Although it presents complex issues, Revelation is the Word of God, and it comes with an attached blessing for those who read and hear its words (1:3).

Interpretation as Faith

Revelation requires from its reader an unusual commitment. We must approach all of Scripture with the mind of faith, believing that Scripture is the very Word of God, accepting its sufficiency, adequate clarity, and value for us. But to these necessary preconditions Revelation adds a layer of complexity. Conservatives hold multiple distinct methods of interpretation for this book. The images in Revelation paint such an unfamiliar picture of the future that readers must assess whether it is predominantly symbolic or literal. Since the events of Revelation seem to occur in the future, who can guarantee that his interpretation is correct? The spiritual interpreter can assign his spiritual meanings to the text (and who can question such lofty, eminently applicable spiritual truths?), and the literal interpreter can insist on literal meanings for the text (and who doubts that God reveals His Word clearly and consistently?) without fear of absolute contradiction since we cannot assay the

[1] See chapter 2 for definitions of these terms.

quality of a future event. Interpreters can always reject an opposing perspective as "impossible," "unnatural," or "unspiritual."

In short, each interpretive system uses vocabulary and argumentation that exhibits its confidence, its "faith," in the rightness of its methodology, the superiority of its explanatory power, and the coherence of its system. Adherence to a particular method of interpretation is a matter of faith. At times, writers defend their system of interpretation with the same aggressive firmness we might expect to see when someone challenges faith. Some writers even anathematize their opponents as heterodox for daring to postulate a different method.

Our culture responds to such clashes of interpretations with an insistent tolerance. Sometimes it supplants these faiths with another: since faiths clash, they must all be wrong. That conclusion defies logic and sets up its own standard of belief. Some interpretation of Revelation must be true—this doesn't mean we have arrived at it fully yet—and this requires competing interpretations to be less accurate and contradicting interpretations to be false. But the church has long assessed the interpretation of prophecy as too fraught with problems and questions to warrant *the same degree of confidence* as other doctrines. That Christ is coming again and will reign forever, we all agree. Until that time we must interpret, hold to our interpretations, and study and make sense of prophecy with a growing understanding. It will do no good to pretend that we don't hold to a particular interpretation system. It will also do no good to pretend that we have all the answers. We interpret as consistently as we are able, but we also believe that our interpretation is correct and true.

Need for This Book

Eschatology (the study of last things) remains the ugly stepsister in theological study. Many Christians treat prophecy as indecipherable. The doctrines of God the Father, Christ, sin, salvation, and the church overshadow eschatology, which is forced into the back seat of biblical study. After all, redemption in time must precede glories in the future, and the business of salvation in this age of opportunity demands our attention. But eschatology is the fruit and fulfillment of all other doctrines. It is not disconnected, irrelevant speculation on the unknown. Eschatology concerns itself with what the Bible reveals about Christ's activity in the future. It discerns what the Bible says about the end of sin, the final outcome of our salvation, and the end state of Israel and the church. What God has revealed about the future presents the fullness of His plan and the end goal of many doctrines. Without it, we would be sorely impoverished as a people of God. Since the Bible reveals so much about the future, God apparently considers the topic important for His people in the present age. We are not acting biblically when we treat a large portion of God's Word as unnecessary, incomprehensible, or theologically inferior. Those who put the study of the future in its proper place are not fools or doomsdayers. They are acting as God has intended. Eschatology is a significant part of God's revelation. He stamps our study with His approval.

Sharp divisions still exist over the interpretation of Revelation.[2] By the law of non-contradiction, they cannot all be correct interpretations. The people of God ought to search for truth so that they may unite behind God's purposes. The rising popularity of

[2] For example, the entire issue of *Southern Baptist Journal of Theology* 14, no. 1 (Spring 2010), argues against a literal fulfillment of prophecy and a literal interpretation of Revelation. I believe the claims that its articles make are unwarranted and fraught with logical fallacies, but it illustrates the variance that still exists in interpreting prophecy.

the young Reformed movement has led to a resurgence in symbolic interpretation and Amillennialism. The Reformers did not, as many of their followers assume, treat eschatology extensively or prove Amillennialism to be the correct biblical interpretation. They simply assumed it from the theology of Roman Catholicism. God placed Luther, Calvin, and their immediate successors in a position to bring vital truths concerning man, sin, and salvation to the forefront of theology. We should recognize their lack of attention to the field of eschatology, and we should not allow their positions to drive present theological discussion. Their periodic comments on the future do not deserve unquestioning loyalty.

The persistence of doctrinal abuses within the various systems of interpretation calls for a careful reevaluation of Revelation. From the abuses by futurists, such as Harold Camping, who wish to attach the book directly to their day, to the heterodoxy of consistent preterists like John Noē, who deny that any Second Coming of Christ or resurrection of believers remains in the future, unbiblical interpretations and unbiblical applications persist. The church needs to understand Revelation better in order to avoid eschatological pitfalls as it avoids Christological ones.

Since Revelation discloses Christ Himself, our study possesses inherent value. God did not reveal the future in abstract terms for abstract reasons. He gave us hundreds of verses on eschatology to reveal the person, character, and actions of the Son. We should study these verses, compare passages, set events in their biblically revealed order, look for connections, and admire the Christ Who comes in power and glory. Such study brings praise and honor to the God Who knows the future and declares the end from the beginning. Revelation has significant practical value. The knowledge and application of eschatology is one part of our worship of

God. Hebrews 11:6 tells us that God rewards "them that diligently seek him," and the search for Christ in eschatology is no different from the search for Him in the rest of the Bible. Eschatology deserves serious investigation and careful comparing of the whole counsel of Scripture. We should not laud those who exercise extreme diligence and careful reconciliation of passages concerning salvation while scorning those who exercise the same kind of diligence and care concerning eschatology.

Purpose of This Book

This book does not pretend to solve all interpretive problems. It expresses decisively my own conviction concerning the interpretation of Revelation. The predominantly literal method of interpretation that leads to a futurist, premillennial position is correct. It simply has greater warrant than its competitors.

On the other hand, this book may not persuade some people to abandon their previously held positions. Since previously held theological positions often drive the interpretation of prophecy, those who place their confidence in a non-literal method of interpretation may not find my case convincing. Persuasion is not the book's primary purpose. Nor do I intend merely to "preach to the choir" of literal interpreters. The goal of this book is both more modest and more ambitious. I hope to guide the student, pastor, and teacher in making important interpretive decisions in Revelation, to provide them with an adequate warrant for their decision, and to buttress their confidence against those who offer a contrary method of interpretation. This book addresses the most crucial issues of interpretation that lead to the various systems. It provides a reasonable defense for the literal method, for Premillennialism, and for a Christ-centered focus on the book of Revelation.

In some areas this book marks an advance in knowledge and presentation. The argument for the prophetic nature of Revelation, in particular, adduces some new evidence you are not likely to see elsewhere. The defense of a predominantly literal method also contributes by its breadth of argumentation. The chapter on Christology may help the reader see in Revelation a value that he has not seen before. In other areas, this book represents a condensation and a distillation of a few key ideas. The chapter on the Millennium fits this description. Some of the sections on the major systems extract and chart what the reader could find elsewhere, but these sections help the reader by condensing extensive research into a more reader-friendly format.

Constructive Outline

In order to accomplish these goals, the book unfolds in a fashion that builds upon the arguments that precede a given chapter. Although the reader may choose to study a given chapter in isolation, that chapter likely refers to a preceding argument.

The most foundational question of interpretation is whether to interpret symbolically or literally. Chapter 1 and appendix 1 address these concerns. Chapter 2 shows how the major systems (Preterism, Historicism, Idealism, and Futurism) build on their chosen method of interpretation. Chapter 3 treats the millennial positions. These too relate to both a particular interpretive method and particular system. Chapter 4 turns to the person of Christ. He is the focus of Revelation. His is the glory. Chapter 5 addresses some of the purposes for which the book exists. It also answers a few crucial questions that arise in the course of eschatology and Revelation.

1

A Case for Literal Interpretation

When my wife and I bought a new game for our children, my son, who was four years old, ripped open the bag containing the pieces and started marching them all over the game board. Chaos ensued as he tried to dive right into the gift while his older sister sought order and procedure. She insisted on reading the rules and following them meticulously. That did not sit well with her free-spirited brother. Both seemed to the other to be "perverting" the intent of the game, which is to have fun. Although I could appreciate their different expressions of enthusiasm, I never intended for the gift to cause conflict. My daughter had the proper *procedure*, even though my son's more holistic approach reflected a proper *attitude* toward the gift. I intervened to stop the war. Then I read the rules to both of them and showed them how to play. Rules must ground any sensible use of a game. Similarly, when God entrusts man with the gift of written Scripture, we must learn how the rules of language work in order to use His gift properly. This is the reason that we will spend these first two chapters addressing the foundational issue of *hermeneutics*. This word simply means "the rules by which we interpret written communication properly."

Hermeneutics texts often provide a list of procedures and principles so that we can understand an author correctly. Most of these books address the relationship between literal and figurative communication. Many provide specific principles such as (1) interpret literally unless the context clearly indicates a figurative use; (2) interpret literally unless the literal meaning contradicts other parts of the canon; and (3) interpret literally unless the literal image produces an absurdity or impossibility.

When these books turn to the topic of interpreting prophecy, they suddenly diverge. Some defend a literal interpretation. Others argue that symbolism predominates and should be considered the normal interpretation. Conflict erupts, and neither position can prove the literalness or figurativeness of a future event. Both sides remain devoted to their presuppositions and their interpretations. Table 1 illustrates some of these presuppositions and arguments. I have tried to align each argument with its corresponding counterargument so that the reader can grasp quickly how each interpretive method responds to the other. The last line shows that theological conservatives sponsor both sides. Pitting champions of conservative beliefs against each other results in a stalemate. If progress is to occur, it must do so in the four points of conflict.

Table 1—Arguments for Literal & Figurative Hermeneutics

Literal Hermeneutic	Figurative Hermeneutic
Language is predominantly literal. No warrant exists for the claim that symbols predominate in prophecy.	Natural language uses symbols. Symbols predominate in prophecy.
No warrant exists for a shift in interpretive method. Prophetic genre does not change overall interpretive method.	Taking Revelation as an apocalypse warrants the interpretive shift. A new genre demands a new method.
Fulfilled prophecy confirms a literal interpretation.	A NT spiritual interpretation of the OT confirms the spiritual interpretive method.
An essentially linear structure in Revelation provides the most natural connection between the events and yields a literal method.	A recapitulatory structure in Revelation requires symbolic interpretation since a literal method no longer works.
Many theological conservatives hold this view.	Many theological conservatives hold this view.

Interpreters on both sides of the debate concur that the book of Revelation contains some symbols. The mere presence of figurative speech does not raise serious debate. Rather, conflict arises in the adoption of a symbolic or literal interpretive *method*. This chapter defends natural literalism as the best method of interpretation. In addition, appendix 1 provides a thorough examination and treatment of the symbolic method of interpretation.

Basis for Literal Interpretation

The history of interpretation, a proper procedure in logic, and a consistent hermeneutic provide strong support for literal interpretation. The following sections examine each of these ideas in turn.

The Historical Argument—Observing the Earliest Interpretation[1]

Not all interpreters comment on the history of Revelation's interpretation, but those who do examine evidence from the early church conclude that the earliest fathers held to a literal, earthly, millennial conception that can derive only from a literal method of interpretation.[2] Some literal interpreters assume that this provides

[1] See the section entitled "The Historical Argument for Symbolic Interpretation" in appendix 1 for a fuller development of this evidence.

[2] Robert H. Mounce lists Justin Martyr, Irenaeus, and Hippolytus as examples. *No* earlier church fathers support the symbolic method, which did not appear until the time of the Alexandrian school. *The Book of Revelation*, rev. ed., The New International Commentary on the New Testament, ed. Gordon D. Fee (Grand Rapids: Eerdmans, 1998), 24–25. The broad scope of literature on Revelation backs his conclusion. See Grant R. Osborne, *Revelation*, Baker Exegetical Commentary on the New Testament, ed. Moisés Silva (Grand Rapids: Baker Academic, 2002), 20; Henry Barclay Swete, *The Apocalypse of St John* (Macmillan and Co., 1906; repr., Eugene, OR: Wipf and Stock Publishers, 1998), cciii–cciv; R. H. Charles, *A Critical and Exegetical Commentary on the Revelation of St John*, vol. 1, The International Critical Commentary, ed. S. R. Driver, A. Plummer, and C. A. Briggs (1950; repr., Edinburgh: T & T Clark, 2000), clxxxiv. See also David O. Beale, "Ante-Nicene Eschatology" (PhD diss., Bob Jones University, 1980) as well as Paul Lee Tan, *The Interpretation of Prophecy* (Winona Lake, IN: BMH Books, 1974), 67–69.

adequate warrant for the system against any counterproposal, but history is not so much prescriptive as it is descriptive. Historical observation vitiates the claim that Premillennialism and a literal interpretation are novelties in the history of the church, but it cannot absolutely prove the method to be valid and correct. History simply indicates that the earliest church fathers applied the literal method to Revelation. At the same time, it cannot be denied that the earliest interpretation of Revelation was a literal interpretation. Those who should have been in the best position to know what the book meant did not treat it symbolically or allegorically.

The Logical Argument—Placing the Burden of Proof Properly

A symbolic method of interpretation tries to shift the burden of proof off of itself and onto literal interpretation. It typically plays the trump card of apocalyptic literature to accomplish this shift.[3] Since asserting Revelation's apocalyptic quality seems to be an overstated assumption, literal interpreters have every right to reject the shifting of this burden of proof and to insist that a symbolic method establish itself as unequivocally superior *before* the interpreter accepts its validity.[4] It has not done so at present.

In the current state of theological study, the interpreter's shift from a literal to a symbolic method depends more on his personal theological system than on evidence warranting such a shift. We cannot escape our assumptions entirely, but the normal, grammatical-historical method of interpretation minimizes the interpreter's assumptions by following standard procedures of interpretation rather than appealing to a new method, which conveniently backs what the interpreter already believes. Logically, the

---

[3] See appendix 1, "The Genre Argument—Revelation as Apocalyptic" for a thorough discussion of this topic and for argumentation in favor of Revelation's prophetic quality.

[4] Robert L. Thomas, *Revelation 1–7* (Chicago: Moody Press, 1992), 24–28.

burden of proof ought to remain on the symbolic method until it can adduce enough evidence to warrant overturning the literal method.

The Hermeneutical Arguments

The previous argument gains greater credibility when we realize that the interpreters who defend a symbolic interpretation of Revelation typically insist that a literal, grammatical-historical method of interpretation must apply to the rest of Scripture.[5] In other words they apply their system of interpretation inconsistently.

Proper interpretation requires that the exegete recognize the correct meaning of words in their contexts. In order to do this, he must operate under the assumption that the natural meaning is the correct meaning unless the context strictly forbids it or the writer indicates another meaning.[6] Although some symbols occur in Revelation, nothing in the context warrants the assumption that most of the words in the book are symbols. If we apply that type of methodology and reasoning to the sermons and predictions of Christ in Scripture, we destroy the Gospels entirely, just as the allegorists did. Examine John 2:13–21 as an example. Jesus cleanses the temple. The Jews ask for a sign of His authority, and He replies, "Destroy this temple, and in three days I will raise it up." The context interprets the symbol *temple* as referring to His body. Imagine that we now reason, "Since this was symbolic, so was Jesus' cleansing of the temple. Oxen appear in the Old Testament under the

[5] The substantial works on hermeneutics by Berkhof, Terry, and Osborne serve as excellent examples. In each case the recognition that some symbolism does exist in Revelation somehow transforms into the belief that symbolism is the driving force of the book. At that point the interpreter has crossed the line from literal to symbolic interpretation.

[6] While it is true that the most apparent, basic meaning of a word may differ from its actual meaning in usage (*usus loquendi*), one cannot assume that a given usage differs from the ordinary meaning unless he establishes this difference from context.

brazen altar; so if people are selling oxen, they must be repudiating God's divine wrath and the necessity of sacrifice. Sheep are dumb, helpless animals. They represent the poor of the land. Jesus is obviously castigating the rulers for abusing the poor." A fertile imagination can both create such figurative connections and defend them as more "spiritual" than the literal meaning. The context, however, does not permit changing the meaning of the words into something other than their natural meaning even though one clear symbol does appear in that context.

Daniel's narrative, which serves spiritual interpreters as the chief ground from the Old Testament for taking Revelation symbolically, actually argues against the symbolic interpretation of everything except its contextually evident symbols. Daniel 2 serves as a clear example. Everything in the report of events is straightforwardly literal until verse 31. Verses 31–35 give the vision that Nebuchadnezzar had literally dreamed. The interpretation in verses 36–45 is both literal and specific—pertaining to specific people, specific empires, specific chronology, and specific consequences. There is no warrant for a spiritual method of interpretation. Literal interpretation recognizes that symbols exist. It allows the context to interpret those symbols, but it insists that the natural interpretation of the remaining contextual images and events is literal.

Interpretation must proceed from the known to the unknown. If we build our case for a favored hermeneutical principle on disputed uses, we blunt the force of our argument and weaken its value for proving our point.

Scripture Indicates and Interprets Symbols

Many exegetes have observed that Scripture regularly (1) indicates when symbols appear in prophecy and (2) interprets those symbols for the prophet.[7] This fact implies that symbolic communication was the exception, not the rule, and that neither the prophets nor the recipient communities had a special key for unlocking such symbols apart from God's explicit defining of the symbols in His revelation. Table 2 illustrates the internal, contextual interpretation that regularly appears with symbols.[8] Zechariah receives special attention since it is one of the most intensely visionary books outside of Revelation. Even in Zechariah most of the book's content is directly literal or ethical rather than symbolic. Where symbolism appears without a divine interpretation (such as Rev. 12:1–3), speculation abounds, and consensus in interpretation fails. A proliferation of such symbolism in a single book would make its meaning unintelligible and its interpretation impossible.

Table 2—The Use & Interpretation of Symbols in Scripture

Symbol	Interpretation
Jer. 1:11—an almond tree	Jer. 1:12—watchfulness to perform His Word
Jer. 1:13—a boiling pot facing from the north	Jer. 1:14–16—destruction coming from the north
Jer. 24:1–2—good and bad figs	Jer. 24:5–10—people destined for captivity and ruin
Ezek. 37:1–10—valley of dry bones	Ezek. 37:11–14—people of Israel restored
Dan. 4:4–21—Nebuchadnezzar's tree cut down	Dan. 4:22–26—Nebuchadnezzar would go insane

[7] See D. S. Russell, *The Method and Message of Jewish Apocalyptic* (Philadelphia: Westminster Press, 1964), 162–63. One writer noted, "The symbols employed in the Book of Daniel are, happily, so fully explained that there need be no serious doubt as to the import of most of them." Milton S. Terry, *Biblical Hermeneutics: A Treatise on the Interpretation of the Old and New Testaments*, 2nd ed. (Grand Rapids: Zondervan, n.d.), 262.

[8] This table does not provide an exhaustive list of the symbols in Scripture or an exhaustive list of interpreted symbols. It merely illustrates the internal interpretation that occurs frequently when a symbol appears in Scripture.

Symbol	Interpretation
Dan. 7:3–8, 11–12—four beasts in order	Dan. 7:16–27—four kingdoms in order
Amos 8:1—basket of ripe fruit	Amos 8:2—imminent destruction and the end
Zech. 1:8—man on red horse, other horses in ravine	Zech. 1:10–11—servants of God to patrol the earth
Zech. 1:18—four horns	Zech. 1:19—enemies who scattered Israel
Zech. 1:20—four craftsmen	Zech. 1:21—those who destroy the four horns
Zech. 3:8–9—stone with 7 eyes	Zech. 4:10—eyes of the Lord
Zech. 4:2–3—lampstand and two olive trees	Zech. 4:6–14—Spirit of God and two anointed ones
Zech. 5:1–2—flying scroll	Zech. 5:3—a curse to destroy the evildoers
Zech. 5:6–7—ephah with lead cover and woman	Zech. 5:8—wickedness
Zech. 5:9–10—two women with wings taking the ephah	Zech. 5:11—those who worship the woman in 5:7
Zech. 6:1–3—red, black, white, and dappled horses	Zech. 6:5—four spirits who stand before God
Zech. 11:4—flock doomed to slaughter	Zech. 11:6—inhabitants of the land
Rev. 1:12, 16—seven lampstands and stars	Rev. 1:20—seven churches and their angels
Rev. 12:3—a great red dragon	Rev. 12:9—the devil, Satan, the deceiver
Rev. 20:2—a dragon, the old serpent	Rev. 20:2—the devil, Satan

The use of introductory words or phrases to indicate symbolism coupled with frequently "signposted" figures of speech such as simile seems to give credibility to the argument that God usually indicates where He uses symbols in Scripture. In Revelation alone,

John uses the particle "as" (ὡς) seventy-one times in order to tell us that something in what he saw of the future lay beyond his ability to articulate completely. None of these considerations contradict the literal method of interpretation since a literal interpretation allows for such figures. What they deny is the probability that God would communicate an entire book through symbols (1) without explicitly indicating such a radical shift in hermeneutic from the rest of Scripture and (2) without providing an interpretation or key to understand that book.

Scripture Limits Symbols

The fact that the Bible regularly interprets its symbols gives the exegete a foundation upon which to build his understanding of how God uses symbols. He finds that symbols have limited scope. Even within a given chapter, widespread and uninterpreted use is rare. For example, Daniel's prophecy would cause no problem for the liberal if it were not so detailed. If Daniel 11 communicated even a significant portion of its message through symbolism, it would pose no threat to anti-supernaturalism. The reason liberals have to re-date the book from the sixth century to the second is that while the beasts are symbolic, their actions are not. The events in Daniel appear so clearly, so precisely, and so literally that their referents are unmistakable. And the liberal rejects the existence of a God Who actually knows the future and Who supernaturally communicates that future to His chosen prophets. If Daniel were entirely symbolic, or if even the immediate context around a symbol were symbolic, liberals would have nothing to fear. Nothing in the text could be linked with any precision to anything real in the world, and the prophecy would pass as some idealist, mystical, symbolic prognostication of general events of good versus evil. That is exactly the claim that the spiritual/symbolic method

makes about Revelation. Since Daniel and Revelation are unquestionably similar in tone, genre, and content, if Daniel's symbolism has a limited extent, it is likely that Revelation's would as well.

Observing the Fulfillment of Prophecy

Another useful argument in favor of a literal method proceeds from the fact that it seems unlikely that God would substitute a new hermeneutic without warning or indication that He did so, applicable to no other book of Scripture, and in place of a method that He used for sixty-five other books. Many writers agree:

> History answers the most important question in prophetic interpretation, that is, whether prophecy is to be interpreted literally, by giving five hundred examples of precise literal fulfillments. The commonly held belief that prophecy is not literal and should be interpreted nonliterally has no basis in scriptural revelation.[9]

> There is not a single prophecy, of which the fulfillment is recorded in Scripture, that was not realized with absolute accuracy, and in every detail; and it is wholly unjustifiable to assume that a new system of fulfillment was inaugurated after the sacred canon closed.[10]

The bulk of prophecy known to have been fulfilled so far had a literal fulfillment. Literal interpreters regularly utilize this fact as decisive evidence for their method. Spiritual interpreters balk and produce a few, select counterexamples, but the argument of the

---

[9] John F. Walvoord, *Prophecy in the New Millennium: A Fresh Look at Future Events* (Grand Rapids: Kregel Publications, 2001), 11.

[10] Robert Anderson, *The Coming Prince*, 14th ed. (Grand Rapids: Kregel Publications, 1954), 147.

literal interpreter holds.[11] The fact that prophecy has had a literal fulfillment is so astonishingly clear that even the amillennialist William Cox can wax eloquent,

> Jeremiah predicted (c. 626 B.C.) that Israel would go into captivity, and that after seventy years she would be returned to Palestine. Jerusalem fell to the Babylonians in 586 B.C. However, the actual captivity consisted of three waves, with the first group going into captivity in 606 B.C. Cyrus' decree came in 537–36, so that Jeremiah's seventy years were literally fulfilled. Oh the majesty of God's prophecies and their sure fulfillments.[12]

The spiritual interpreter insists that the value of such an event lies in its *surety* rather than its *literality* of fulfillment, but he cannot help but admit the literal fulfillment.

Can we not imagine the symbolic interpreter in Jeremiah's own day saying, "Seventy years? That's 7 x 10. That's the number of perfection times the number of completion. Clearly this is a symbol for God's divine superintendence over Jerusalem that will prevent its physical, national captivity (since according to our system, there is no way God will abandon His temple to pagan interference or Jerusalem to destruction)." Cox admits this kind of rationale when he claims that "numerology, imagery, etc., are not meant to be ends within themselves. Rather they are to be only means to an end, i.e., to get across the central truth God has for

---

[11] See appendix 1, "The New Testament's Spiritual Application of the Old," for a discussion and refutation of the passages that symbolic interpreters use to justify their position.

[12] William E. Cox, *Amillennialism Today* (Philadelphia: Presbyterian and Reformed Publishing Company, 1966), 39.

His people."[13] But unless we knew preemptively what that "central truth" was, we could not interpret the symbol. At this point the presuppositions of the figurative interpreter enter. He assumes that the "central point" *cannot* pertain to Israel, an earthly kingdom of Christ, or the literal fulfillment of prophecy. And once he demands a symbolic meaning, no one can contradict his conclusions without seeming to be irrational. The syllogism is essentially as follows:

> P¹—Revelation communicates predominantly through symbols.
> P²—The central meaning of Revelation pertains to the church, not Israel.
> ∴—Premillennialism/Futurism cannot be the correct interpretation of the book.

Logically, the premillennialist and futurist must attack one or both of the premises in order to undermine the conclusion. The evidence from the fulfillment of prophecy undermines the first premise. The nature of God's covenants with Israel undermines the second.[14] Table 3 provides a series of literally fulfilled prophecies for consideration. The table does not indicate a ratio of figurative to literal fulfillment. Interpreters cannot form such a ratio since they cannot reach agreement in every case, but the evidence from the Old Testament is clear: prophecy finds a predominantly literal fulfillment.[15]

---

[13] Ibid., 65.

[14] See appendix 1, "The Nature of Biblical Covenants" and "Problems with a Symbolic View of Biblical Covenants," for evidence backing this assertion.

[15] The counterexamples to a literal interpretation of prophecy offered by George Eldon Ladd, "Historic Premillennialism," in *The Meaning of the Millennium: Four Views*, ed. Robert G. Clouse (Downers Grove, IL: IVP Academic, 1977), 22–24, are not convincing. The easiest interpretation in each case is still a straightforward, literal interpretation. The fact that the NT adds greater specificity to the OT prophecy when fulfilling it in Christ does not revoke the literalness of the prophecy. Thus, while Isaiah 53 does not say "Messiah" directly, it is absurd to claim (as Ladd does) that it was, therefore, not fulfilled

Table 3—Select Prophecies Fulfilled Literally

Prophecy	Fulfillment
2 Sam. 7:12–13—David's son would build a temple	1 Kings 8:15–24—Solomon built the temple
1 Kings 11:29–40—Jeroboam to rule 10 tribes	1 Kings 12:15
1 Kings 13:1–2—birth of Josiah, who would burn the false priests' bones at Bethel	2 Kings 23:15–16 (300 years later)
1 Kings 14:10—Jeroboam's line would cease	1 Kings 15:29 (>2 years later)
1 Kings 21:23—Jezebel to be eaten by dogs	2 Kings 9:35–37 (20 years later)
2 Kings 7:1–2—readily available food w/in 24 hours; official would see it but not eat of it	2 Kings 7:17–20—food available w/in 24 hours; official saw it but was trampled to death before he ate
Ps. 22:7–18—Messiah mocked in reference to His confidence in God Thirsting Pierced in hands and feet Clothing divided by lot	Matt. 27:41–43 "He trusted in God; let him deliver him now, if he will have him" John 19:28 "that the scripture might be fulfilled" John 20:25 "the print of the nails" John 19:24 "that the scripture might be fulfilled"
Ps. 34:20—bones not broken	John 19:33–37 "that the scripture should be fulfilled"
Isa. 7:14—a virgin conceiving, the child named Immanuel	Matt. 1:22–23 "All this was done, that it might be fulfilled which was spoken of the Lord by the prophet"
Isa. 9:1–2—Naphtali/Galilee receiving a great light through Messiah (9:6)	Matt. 4:13–16 "That it might be fulfilled which was spoken by Esaias the prophet"

literally but figuratively in Jesus Christ. With this kind of plasticity of interpretation, nothing could be fulfilled literally unless every detail of the later event was spelled out in advance (a procedure that would require massive volumes of literature). There is a significant difference between a later event's failing to meet the actual provisions of the earlier prophecy and the later event's adding more details to the fulfillment of that prophecy. The first, which *is not* the model that Scripture follows, would warrant spiritual interpretation. The second, which *is* the pattern of Scripture, demands a literal interpretation.

Prophecy	Fulfillment
Isa. 44:28—Cyrus would decree the rebuilding	Ezra 1:1—Cyrus decreed the return to Jerusalem and the rebuilding of the temple
Jer. 25:1–12; 29:10—70-year captivity	Dan. 9:1–3—Daniel recognized the 70 years as literal and as nearly complete
Dan. 4:24–26—the king would go insane	Dan. 4:33—Nebuchadnezzar went insane
Dan. 11—Persian kings, rise of Greece, division of Greek empire, wars of Ptolemies and Seleucids, rise of Antiochus Epiphanes who would defile the temple	Secular history confirms the events in minute detail; occurred several hundred years later
Mic. 5:2—Bethlehem as Messiah's birthplace	Matt. 2:5–6 "Thus it is written by the prophet"
Nah. 1:8, 14; 2:6–10; 3:15–19—Nineveh to be totally overthrown, besieged, flooded	Secular history confirms the events in detail; occurred in 612 BC (20 years later)
Zech. 12:10—looked upon by those who pierced Him	John 19:37 "another scripture saith, They shall look on him whom they pierced"

Treating Figures of Speech in Revelation

A literal method admits the existence of symbols since a literal method simply assumes that language follows its natural patterns—patterns that can draw upon figures of speech. How then can the interpreter proceed? There are well-founded means for discerning between a literal referent and a figurative one.

Recognizing Symbols

The debate over the meaning, frequency, and use of symbols marks a hotly contested battleground in interpreting Revelation. All honest interpretive positions seek the meaning of the text. Literal interpretation focuses on the words of the text while recognizing symbols. Symbolic interpretation asserts the existence of a spiritual meaning behind the words while recognizing words.

A symbol is different from other figures of speech. It is a special class of comparison that communicates a deeper meaning than the superficial word or image.[16] Metaphors typically convey a similarity between two objects. "Love is an ocean" serves as a good example. The thought is not "an ocean symbolizes love" so much as it is "Love is deep, broad, and unfathomable." Compare this with the statement, "[I] saw a beast rise up out of the sea, having seven heads and ten horns" (Rev. 13:1). The image in Revelation does not invite the same type of comparison that the ordinary metaphor did. It does not expect the reader to ask the question *how do these things relate* so much as *what does this represent*? A metaphor says "X is Y," while a symbol simply says "Y." Once a writer interprets a symbol for his reader, it becomes more nearly metaphorical in force. So when John refers to the "great red dragon" (12:3) and then explains the symbol as representing "that old serpent, called the Devil, and Satan, which deceiveth the whole world" (12:9), the reader now has "Satan is a great red dragon" in the stock of figures in his mind.

As the frequency and proximity of symbols to each other increase, the probability of figuring out what those symbols mean decreases. We need an adequate explanatory context to figure out what a symbol means. For instance, if I were to communicate in the following fashion, you would probably not understand what I meant: "The stars, diving from their courses, stalked the abyss when Mars strode in the hamlet of the Dutch."[17] On the other hand, if a writer surrounds a symbol with normal communication

[16] In some sense a symbol is an implied, cumulative-force metaphor. It is an implied metaphor because the "X is" portion of the "X is Y" statement remains tacit. It has cumulative force because a symbol rarely evokes a single point of comparison. It is still a metaphor because it relates two objects to each other figuratively.

[17] Check your interpretation. I meant, "A US flag fell from a flag-bearer's hand onto the ground at the Battle of Gettysburg."

(the way symbols typically appear in literature), the interpretation of that symbol becomes more feasible. For instance, "My pony may not be pretty, but she gets good gas mileage and her insurance is cheap." This observation provides a fairly strong warrant for the use of the literal method of interpretation in Revelation. Either the book lies beyond our ability to interpret, and its value decreases in direct proportion to its incomprehensibility, or its symbolism is of such a nature and limited frequency that we can understand for the most part what its events mean. An affirmation of the predominantly symbolic nature of the book is a vote in favor of incoherence. Any interpretation whatsoever might be true, and no one is capable of disputing the interpretation on rational grounds. This is one reason that a symbolic interpretation of the book has yielded ideas as diverse as Amillennialism, Postmillennialism, Preterism, Historicism, and Idealism.

Several interpretive principles help us recognize when we are facing a symbol.[18]

1. Obviously a symbol exists if the writer interprets his own statements as such (Rev. 1:20; 4:5).
2. If the image lies outside the bounds of reason, a symbol may be in view (Rev. 3:12).
3. If other Scripture passages interpret the same image as a symbol, warrant may exist for doing so in this passage as well (cf. Rev. 1:16 with Heb. 4:12; cf. Rev. 9:1 with 1:20).

---

[18] See the lengthier analysis in Brian R. Hand, *The Worthy Champion: A Christology of the Book of Revelation Based on Elements of Its Literary Composition* (Greenville, SC: Bob Jones University Press, 2008), 208–29, from which this section derives. See also the treatment in G. K. Beale, *The Book of Revelation: A Commentary on the Greek Text,* The New International Greek Testament Commentary, ed. I. Howard Marshall and Donald A. Hagner (Grand Rapids: Eerdmans, 1999), 55–58.

4. If the image in question relates closely to another symbol in the passage, it may be symbolic (Rev. 12:1—if the woman clothed with the sun is a symbol, might not the moon and stars be as well?). The interpreter must use this rule guardedly; otherwise he will multiply the number of symbols unnecessarily and make the passage unintelligible.

5. Common physical imagery applied to an unusual referent or to an indisputably spiritual truth may indicate a symbol (Rev. 3:15–16; 3:18). This use matches Jesus' use of parables. Here, too, the interpreter must proceed with extreme caution. Typically, he should not see a symbol in a common image unless the image also fits another one of these rules for determining symbolism. For example, the "hot"-ness and "cold"-ness of the Laodicean church actually receives contextual interpretation ("because you say, 'I am . . .'"). We know it is a symbol not on the basis of its commonality alone but because of its interpretation in the context.

6. A symbol usually cannot serve as a symbol for another symbol. Some writers interpret not only the explicit symbol in Revelation 11:4 (the two candlesticks) as a symbol, but they also interpret its referent (the two witnesses) in Revelation 11:3 as a symbol. This results in an absurdity. The candlesticks are symbolic for the witnesses which are symbolic for . . . what? Those who try to add this second layer of symbolism are exhibiting the use of a spiritual-symbolic method of interpretation rather than a literal method. Where Scripture uses symbols, the referent is real, not additionally symbolic.[19]

[19] Zechariah provides many pertinent examples. The horns (1:18) are those who scattered Judah, Israel, and Jerusalem (1:19). The reader does not find "those who scattered" to be a symbol for anything else. The scattering occurred literally. One exception to this rule might appear in Revelation 17:9–10 where the seven heads

7. Do not impute to an image either symbolic quality (it may not be a symbol) or an unwarranted interpretation (it may not mean what you think) where the text does not directly warrant it. An example of the first error concerns the interpretation of the locust-like creatures from the abyss (Rev. 9). Nothing in the context indicates that these are symbols for anything else. The context does tell us that they are not insects, however. Since we have no personal experience with the abyss, with demonic creatures in the spiritual realm, and with the future, we have no means of deciding conclusively that these are symbolic unless the context tells us that they are (and it does not).[20] The second error examines the same passage, accepts a vague literality to the locust-creatures and then turns them into helicopters. That may provide an interesting speculation, but it has no basis in the text.

Beale adds that a metaphor is evident when "conceptual word boundaries are transgressed."[21] For instance, if a writer conveys, "A star took a key and unlocked the abyss," everything fits proper conceptual categories except for the word *star*. The reader has every warrant to interpret the star as a symbol. He does not have warrant to interpret *key*, *unlock*, or *abyss* as a symbol, however, from this context. This assessment follows normal interpretive rules.[22]

---

of the beast are seven mountains and seven kings. Either the mountains symbolize the kings, or the mountains are a distinct referent from the kings. Both the mountains and the kings could be literal. We have no way of judging this to be a double symbol or simply literal until it comes to pass.

[20] Apparently John initially saw these creatures from a distance. Since they rose up in a cloud, they would appear like locusts. As they drew nearer, he could enter into the sustained description of them that we see in vv. 7–11. In any case the term *locusts* in v. 3 is metaphoric, not symbolic. The creatures really were *like* locusts.

[21] G. K. Beale, 55.

[22] Some interpreters emphasize synchronic study as the single greatest key to unlocking the meaning of symbols in Revelation. Grant R. Osborne, *The Hermeneutical Spiral: A Comprehensive Introduction to Biblical Interpretation* (Downers Grove, IL: InterVarsity

A symbol does not exist merely because the interpreter lacks the ability to explain the text, or the faith to admit the apparent meaning of the text, the awareness of how the text integrates with other Scripture. Thus Boettner's inability to accept the biblical representation of the Millennium does not warrant spiritualizing the passages that contain it:

> That condition, semiheavenly and semiearthly, with Christ reigning—apparently—in Jerusalem, with two radically different types of people (the saints in glorified, resurrected bodies and ordinary mortals still in the flesh mingling freely throughout the world for the long and almost unending period of one thousand years) strikes me as so unreal and impossible that I wonder how anyone can take it seriously.[23]

Unless the interpreter bridles his thinking by using normal hermeneutics and the model that Scripture has already set, his interpretation becomes increasingly tenuous, especially in his treatment of symbols.

Press, 1991), 228–29. Several problems emerge that have led me to omit it as a useful model. First, there are no other first-century canonical books like Revelation. How can we study what John "would have done" when we lack corroborating or contradicting evidence? Second, assuming that John would use the same imagery in the same way as earlier, non-canonical apocalypses is extremely dangerous since even the apocalypses did not use symbols with any consistency. Often the same symbol meant radically different things from one apocalypse to another. Moreover, we have evidence that symbols are not always consistent within Scripture. Consider, for example, the fact that the lion in the Bible could reference Judah, Christ, or Satan. Within Revelation, the stars of chapter 1 are interpreted as the angels of the seven churches, but the star of chapter 9 may not be a holy being at all. Third, the assumption that the church, particularly the Gentiles in the church, would have known or cared about sectarian Jewish mythical literature enough to learn its symbols is dubious.

[23] Loraine Boettner, "Postmillennialism," in *The Meaning of the Millennium: Four Views*, 49.

Other Figures of Speech

Some figures of speech present such an obvious comparison that the reader will not struggle with understanding or applying the figure. For example, we don't need special training to recognize that similes are not expressing literal connections between two words. A simile is an overt comparison using *like* or *as*. Similes abound in Revelation. John describes the hair of the glorified Christ as "white like wool" and his eyes "as a flame of fire" (1:14). Wherever similes occur, they indicate figurative meaning. John does not say that Jesus' hair was wool or that His eyes were a fire. Moreover, even when similes are crowded together in close proximity and high frequency they do not typically create the confusion that symbols do. Similes have a more overt quality of communication than symbols have.

Several other figures of speech do not affect the interpretation so much as they give an interesting "color" to the events. *Epizeuxis*, for example, uses the repetition of a term to draw attention or create emphasis. When an angel cries out, "Babylon is fallen, is fallen," the repetition does not make the event more certain, but it certainly draws attention to the importance of it (Rev. 14:8). *Synecdoche* replaces a whole with its parts or a part with the whole. So when Revelation 1:7 tells us that "all kindreds of the earth shall wail because of him," we know that it refers to individual people within those tribes. *Pleonasm* occurs where a text sets numerous synonyms or near-synonyms side-by-side for emphasis. Usually the reader should not isolate the synonyms and treat them separately. They exist for cumulative effect (though they may have some significance individually as well). A good example appears in Revelation 5:12: "Worthy is the Lamb that was slain to receive power, and riches, and wisdom, and strength, and honour, and glory, and blessing." With *irony* an author states one thing while implying its opposite. One of the best examples of this appears in Revelation 3:17 on the lips of the church of Laodicea: "I am rich, and increased with goods, and have need of nothing." The immediate context indicates the irony, since that very church is "wretched, and miserable, and poor, and blind, and naked." *Hendiadys*, the use of two terms to express the same idea, likely occurs in Revelation 20:10, "the lake of fire and brimstone." The reader senses that fire and brimstone are probably a single concept. None of these other figures of speech create the difficulty for interpreters that symbolism creates. Moreover, all of these figures are parts of natural, normal, literal communication. The interpreter need not jettison the expectation of the literal in order to recognize the figurative where it occurs. However, expecting the non-literal or insisting on seeing a pervasive symbolism jeopardizes proper interpretation by assigning figurative meaning to people, places, events, and ideas that are actually literal in the text.

Summary

Interpreters agree that Revelation contains symbols. They do not agree on the frequency and interpretation of those symbols. A literal method follows established rules of grammar to insist that the bulk of the book is literal while recognizing those elements that are clearly symbolic. A spiritual method departs from established rules of grammar to insist that the bulk of the book is symbolic while admitting a few literal referents. Writers often mourn the fact that the book has remained opaque for centuries of church history, but a spiritual interpretation, which necessarily obscures the meaning of the text, prevailed from Augustine through the Reformers. As soon as the frequency and proximity of symbols increase, the possibility of confident, credible interpretation decreases. A predominantly literal method reopens the possibility of just such a credible interpretation.

Intersection of Hermeneutic and Systems

Where Futurism admits the possibility of either a literal or figurative method, Preterism, Historicism, and Idealism must reject the use of the literal method outright. One cannot interpret literally and arrive at any of these three positions. A presupposition in favor of one of these three systems automatically biases the case against a literal interpretation since these theological systems require a symbolic view of Revelation. In other words, faith in the accuracy of one's theological system can drive the method of interpretation chosen by the interpreter. Obviously, this can also work in reverse: a person can choose a spiritual method and end up at any of the four major interpretive systems. Those who believe an essentially preterist, historicist, or idealist perspective cannot interpret in a neutral fashion without producing dissonance with their chosen system.[24] Figure 1 illustrates the interaction between system and interpretive method.

Figure 1—The Interplay of Method & System

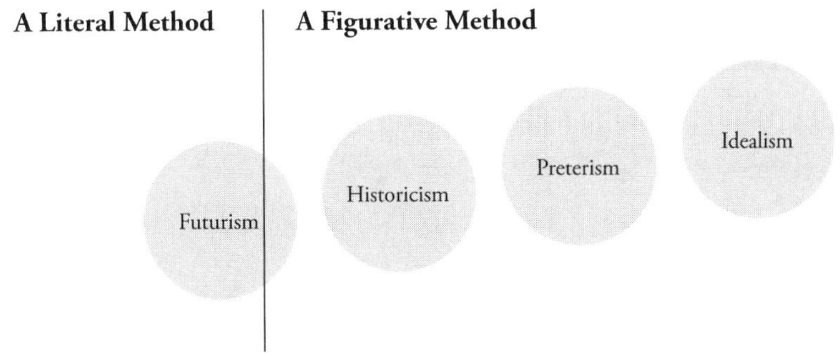

Many writers have observed this phenomenon. Merrill C. Tenney comments, "The more literal an interpretation that one adopts,

[24] This dissonance does occur. Many idealists still believe that Revelation teaches the Second Coming of Christ at the end of the age. For a moment they suspend their system in order to grant what New Testament doctrine clearly teaches. They then return immediately to their symbolism, which does not allow a referent to occur literally in time and space.

the more strongly will he be construed to be a futurist."[25] The fact that a chosen interpretive method can automatically exclude an interpretation that would otherwise be entirely viable should give the interpreter a reason to pause and assess the arguments in favor of literal versus spiritual interpretive systems.

CONCLUSION

Some readers at this point might complain that this insistence on a literal method has not produced a twelve-step method for interpreting Revelation. No lengthy list of special procedures has appeared. This is so precisely because the recognition that Revelation follows a normal, literal method of interpretation means that the same general interpretive principles that apply to the rest of Scripture apply here. The prophetic quality of Revelation coupled with the predominantly literal quality of Old Testament prophecy indicates that the literal method remains superior to a spiritual or symbolic method for interpreting Revelation.

---

[25] Merrill C. Tenney, *Interpreting Revelation: A Reasonable Guide to Understanding the Last Book of the Bible* (1957, Eerdmans; repr., Peabody, MA: Hendrickson Publishers, 2001), 142.

2

Four Major Systems of Interpretation

Since commentators often disagree on the interpretation of the images in Revelation, in order to assess each writer's argument carefully and accurately, you must discern his interpretive position and understand the implications of that position. Four systems prevail as the most significant, broad interpretive options applied to Revelation—Preterism, Historicism, Idealism, and Futurism—and they affect one's perspective on the book significantly. This chapter treats the basic principles of each system, discusses difficulties with each, and presents the case for Futurism as the most coherent of the four systems.

Understanding the Systems

Background

The four major interpretive systems derive from differing answers to two important questions: to what time period do the images in Revelation chapters 4–22 refer?[1] and what kind of referent (literal or symbolic) do the images in Revelation possess?[2] Figure 2 displays the four systems graphically in relation to these two

[1] All of the systems tend to interpret Revelation 1–3 as distinct from the remainder of the book. Historicists and idealists, followed by some futurists, stretch chapters 2–3 into the entire church age with the Laodicean church being the final, apostate church immediately prior to the Second Coming of Christ. The crucial area of disagreement among the systems lies in chapters 4–22.

[2] A *referent* is simply that person, place, event, or object to which the words refer in the intent of the author. In other words, it is "the exact thing signified by the term." Grant R. Osborne, *The Hermeneutical Spiral*, 401.

questions. The figure moves from past to future on the x-axis and from literal to figurative on the y-axis.

Figure 2—Time & Kind of Referent in the Interpretive Systems

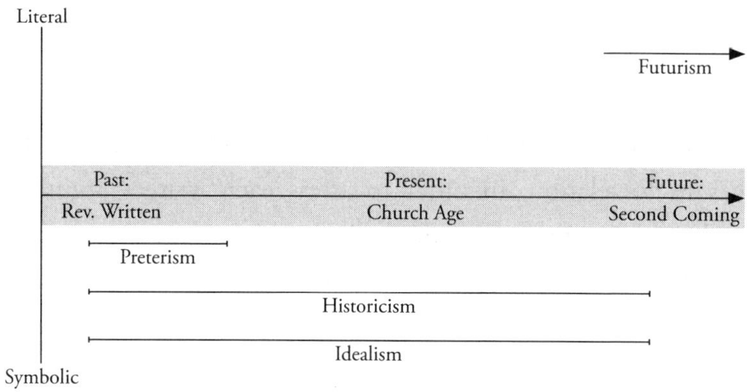

Preterism believes that the images in Revelation occur in the distant past, and it interprets the book symbolically. Historicism and Idealism agree that the book covers the entire church age and that the book is symbolic.[3] They differ, however, on the specificity of the images in Revelation. Historicism believes that the images represent actual events in the course of church history. Idealism rejects any specific, historical referent at all. Instead, it argues that the cumulative force of the images conveys a general sense of the cosmic struggle between good and evil. Futurism defends both the literalness and the futurity of the images in Revelation.[4]

---

[3] Some idealists would reject this description in favor of an atemporal perspective on Revelation. In this view Revelation does not cover even the church age. It is entirely timeless—describing every conflict between good and evil from the primordial fall of Satan into the eternal state. This makes the book eminently relevant to all eras equally, but it also makes the book virtually irrelevant since it would then add nothing to our understanding of any biblical doctrine. The persecuted saint hardly needs a non-referential generality that says simply, "Evil loses, and good wins at various times in various ways with God doing something more or less in the process."

[4] The following discussion omits the extreme forms of all the views. For example, extreme (consistent) Preterism, as represented by J. Stuart Russell, has no place in orthodoxy. It believes that all biblical prophecy, including the second coming of Christ and the final resurrection, has been fulfilled in the destruction of Jerusalem. This is heresy

Preterism is the interpretive system in which (nearly) all the events recorded in Revelation are seen as fulfilled in the events surrounding the destruction of Jerusalem and/or the fall of Rome.[5] Several features characterize the preterist position.[6] First, Preterism insists that the images of Revelation be fulfilled almost immediately following the writing of the book. It claims that since "soon" (τάχος) (1:1; 2:16; 3:11; 22:6, 7, 12, 20) and "near" (ἐγγύς) (1:3; 22:10) appear at several crucial points in Revelation, a soon fulfillment without a delay of years must be in view.[7] For those preterists who believe that the destruction of Jerusalem in AD 70 fulfilled the events of Revelation, the book must have an earlier date than the traditional date in the reign of Domitian (AD 81–96). This has led many to propose a date during the reign of Nero (AD 54–68) as the time of Revelation's writing. Second, recent preterists typically accept Revelation as fitting into the genre of apocalypse. This genre would seem to warrant a figurative interpretation of the

(2 Tim. 2:17–18). Moderate and soft preterists reject such heresy. This book treats only moderates of each position.

[5] Kenneth L. Gentry Jr., F. W. Farrar, and Milton Terry believe the book was fulfilled completely in the fall of Jerusalem. Stuart, Cowles, Scott, and Crafter believe the book was fulfilled partly in the destruction of Jerusalem and partly in the fall of Rome. Some modern preterists have abandoned the fall of Jerusalem as a viable fulfillment (taking the later date for the book) and believe it was exclusively in the fall of Rome.

[6] See Richard Alan Young, "The Interpretation of Revelation" (PhD diss., Bob Jones University, 1981), 40. Young's dissertation provides a thorough examination of these four systems in a scope and depth that we cannot duplicate here. He isolates several tenets of the preterist position as follows: "(1) the nearness of fulfillment, (2) a faithfulness to the historical setting, (3) a purpose of writing to provide comfort for the persecuted, (4) an emphasis on apocalyptic literature, (5) the use of the Nero myth, and (6) the belief in a past fulfillment."

[7] See, for instance, Kenneth L. Gentry Jr., "A Preterist View of Revelation," in *Four Views on the Book of Revelation*, ed. Stanley N. Gundry and C. Marvin Pate (Grand Rapids: Zondervan, 1998), 41. "Language is simply meaningless if it is to be so manipulated by every successive commentator as to make the words 'speedily' and 'near' imply any number of centuries of delay." Frederick W. Farrar, *The Early Days of Christianity* (New York: A. L. Burt, n.d.), 496–97. "'Shortly' can have no other and no less meaning than *very soon*." Henry Cowles, *The Revelation of John* (New York: D. Appleton and Co., 1871), 53.

book. Third, Preterism insists that Revelation must be relevant to its original audience by offering immediate comfort in their time of persecution. Thus, one of Preterism's primary goals is defending the value of Revelation for its original recipients. Additionally, preterists hold amillennial views since the events of Revelation 20 pertain not to the future but to the past.

Historicism

Historicism asserts that the images recorded in Revelation began in the first century and span the entire church age until the Second Coming of Christ. It subdivides into *Continuous Historicism*, which sees the events of Revelation as having a single, specific referent in the events between the two comings of Christ, and *Synchronous Historicism*, which sees the events of Revelation as having multiple general referents in the events between the two comings of Christ. Both of these positions share several features. First, both require a symbolic interpretation of Revelation. For Historicism to have any claim to accuracy, Revelation's events cannot be literal since they have not matched the development of history in any literal way. The modern designation of Revelation as an apocalypse has helped bolster the case for symbolic interpretation, and most historicists would concur that Revelation fits the apocalyptic genre. Second, Historicism believes that early readers could not have understood the interpretation of Revelation. Since the images pertain to future events under a veil of symbolism, it would be impossible to understand the book in the first few centuries of the church's existence. In this view, relevance for the first-century audience sprang from the eternal perspective offered by the book rather than from a promise of a swift judgment of the church's persecutors. In fact, Historicism's third concern is making the book relevant to the entire church age. Historicism developed its strongest following during the Reformation and post-Reformation era, as Christians tried to make sense of intra-church conflicts. Revelation seemed to provide a fitting description of the anti-Christian activities of the Roman Catholic Church and the papacy, and many expositors began looking for connections between Revelation and world events. Fourth, Historicism recognizes that the book of Revelation begins indisputably in the time of the author (chs. 1–3) and ends in the eternal state (chs. 21–22). It contends that the middle portion of the book most naturally fits in the intervening period of earthly history—the church age. Historicism provides a strongly conservative perspective on the book of Revelation since it recognizes the predictive quality of Revelation. Since liberals reject the supernatural (and the predictive capability of Scripture), they do not hold to Historicism. Individual historicists have advocated Amillennialism, Postmillennialism, or Premillennialism.

Idealism

Idealism is the interpretive system that asserts that the images in Revelation have no direct connection to specific, localized persons, places, or events at any point in time. Rather, the book addresses the universal conflict between good and evil.[8] The specific events of Revelation exist for the sake of drama or vividness, not literal accuracy. Several principles undergird this system. First, Revelation is timeless.[9] As a system, Idealism rejects any genuinely predictive

[8] Three defenders of Idealism reason as follows: "While the Apocalypse thus embraces the whole period of the Christian dispensation, it sets before us within this period the action of great principles and not specific events." William Milligan, *Lectures on the Apocalypse* (New York: Macmillan, 1892), 153. "No specific incidents are to be sought for in human history exactly corresponding to the occurrences here depicted." Charles R. Erdman, *The Revelation of John* (Philadelphia: Westminster Press, 1936), 72. "In Revelation words take the place of pigments and brushes to create a portrait designed to visualize great principles, not particular incidents." Sam Hamstra Jr., "An Idealist View of Revelation," in *Four Views on the Book of Revelation*, 97.

[9] "All is unmeasured alike in space and time." E. W. Benson, *The Apocalypse* (London: Macmillan, 1900), 29.

quality in Revelation. There is no fulfillment in any concrete sense since the book predicts nothing other than a general outcome to an ongoing struggle. Its images apply equally well to all generations—past, present, and future. In practice, idealists often abandon the system on isolated incidents in Revelation, such as the Second Coming of Christ. Second, this severing of images from time and place requires a symbolic interpretation of Revelation. Once again, viewing Revelation as an apocalypse serves as one of the chief warrants for this symbolic interpretation. Idealism rejects the literal sense to such an extent that it emphatically *prefers* the symbolic over the literal.[10] Where the literal seems to apply, idealism still denies any attachment to a specific time and place in favor of a general principle. Third, Idealism typically asserts that Revelation's primary purpose is to provide comfort to all believers in their struggle against evil.[11] It recognizes that the book is valuable and applicable to the people of God in the entire church age. Idealists hold an amillennial perspective on the book since the events of Revelation 20 do not match any single, literal time-and-space referent.

Futurism

Futurism is the system of interpretation that views the events of Revelation 4–22 as specific, future events that immediately precede, coincide with, and follow the Second Coming of Christ to earth. Futurism builds on the following tenets. First, most

[10] Even G. K. Beale's modified idealism insists that "the predominant manner by which to approach the material will be according to a nonliteral interpretative method. Of course some parts are not symbolic, but the essence of the book is figurative. Where there is lack of clarity about whether something is symbolic, the scales of judgment should be tilted in the direction of a nonliteral analysis" (52).

[11] This does not imply that all idealists hold to a uniform statement of Revelation's purpose. G. K. Beale believes that the tension between the arrival of Christ's kingdom and the overt reign of evil in the world requires theological explanation (Ibid., 28).

futurists follow a literal hermeneutic.[12] Although some opponents have caricatured this method as slavishly literalistic, a literal interpretation is simply a normal or natural interpretation. It follows the grammatical-historical method as applied to the rest of the Scripture. Second, Futurism typically accepts a single referent for a given image in Revelation. This means that Revelation does not have multiple fulfillments over the ages of history.[13] Third, Futurism recognizes the close connection between Revelation and Old Testament prophecy. This leads some futurists to repudiate the popular conception of Revelation as an apocalypse in favor of its prophetic quality. Fourth, Futurism typically views the victory of Christ as key to the book of Revelation. He brings progressively more destructive judgments against those who reject His authority. He is the Warrior-Lamb, the hope of His people, the King. Although Revelation may comfort God's people, it does so as a byproduct of its real purpose—declaring the vindication and triumph of Christ. Futurists hold either a postmillennial or premillennial view of Revelation since they recognize that if the

---

[12] "A literal rendering of John's language will, of course, result in a futurist view" (Young, 78). "I believe it to be a rule of sound criticism, that we should take the literal sense of every writer, unless sufficient reasons can be given for departing from it". S. R. Maitland, *An Enquiry into the Grounds of Which the Prophetic Period of Daniel and St. John, Has Been Supposed to Consist of 1260 Years* (London: Hatchard and Son, 1826), 2. "If we are to be guided by the fulfillment of the prophecies of the Old Testament concerning the Messiah, and consider how in every case referring to the first advent they have been literally fulfilled, surely no fault ought to be found with those who believe that the direct and positive assertions of God's Word concerning the Second Coming of Christ, as recorded in the Old and New Testaments, will also be literally fulfilled." Revere F. Weidner, *Annotations on the Revelation of St. John the Divine,* The Lutheran Commentary, ed. Henry E. Jacobs (New York: The Christian Literature Co., 1898), xxxv.

[13] This principle does not apply to futurists who also hold to Progressive Dispensationalism. Progressive Dispensationalism allows multiple referents for a given image by accepting an "already/not yet" tension in the New Testament. According to this perspective, a prophecy may have an "already" fulfillment and a "not yet" fulfillment imbedded in the same image. Classic Dispensationalism rejects multiple referents as incoherent and contrary to the pattern of Old Testament prophecy. Only one "fulfillment" can be spoken of as such.

book communicates literal events at all, Amillennialism is impossible. Most futurists are premillennial, a perspective required by Revelation's placing the Second Coming before the Millennium.

Summary

If we compare the beliefs of these positions, several observations emerge. Table 4 below summarizes these positions visually. Notice that Idealism and Historicism align with each other on the time frame covered in Revelation. Preterism, Historicism, and Idealism concur on their interpretive method (symbolic). Although their primary concern differs slightly, these three systems focus on the recipient. Each senses the difficulty in interpreting Revelation and generates a system of thought that will be relevant to the church, whether past or present. All four systems have proponents who assess Revelation as an apocalypse, but Idealism cannot treat it as predictive prophecy, and modern Preterism does not treat it as such. Historicism has largely died out in academic circles in the twentieth century; therefore, no modern proponents appear in the table.[14]

Table 4—A Visual Comparison of the Four Systems

	Preterism	Idealism	Historicism	Futurism
Time Covered in Revelation	Past: First century (through fifth century)	Past–Present: Entire church age, no attachment to specific events	Past–Present: Entire church age, direct attachment to specific events	Future
Method	Symbolic	Symbolic	Symbolic	Literal
Genre	Apocalypse	Apocalypse	Apocalypse or Prophecy	Prophecy or Apocalypse
Structure	Recapitulatory	Recapitulatory	Mixed	Usually linear

[14] "While the historicist approach once was widespread, today, for all practical purposes, it has passed from the scene. Its failed attempts to locate the fulfillment of Revelation in the course of the circumstances of history has [sic] doomed it to a continual

	Preterism	Idealism	Historicism	Futurism
Primary Concern	Relevance to 1st c. audience	Universal spiritual conflict exists, relevance to the entire church age	Relevance to the entire church age	Normal, consistent, literal interpretation to interpret prophecy correctly
Purpose	To steel believers' courage to face persecution	Varies—to comfort persecuted believers	To explain the course of history between the two advents of Christ	To show the eschatological victory of Christ
Millennial Position	Amillennial	Amillennial	Any	Premillennial Postmillennial
Older Proponents	I. T. Beckwith R. H. Charles H. E. Dana F. W. Farrar Milton Terry	H. Alford Augustine W. Hendrickson R. C. H. Lenski Oecumenius	Albert Barnes J. Gill F. Godet A. J. Gordon A. Plummer	D. Barnhouse A. C. Gaebelein H. Ironside Abraham Kuyper Joseph Seiss T. Zahn
Recent Proponents	F. F. Bruce David Chilton Gary DeMar Kenneth Gentry Albertus Pieters J. W. Roberts Ray Summers	G. K. Beale H. Hoeksema William Milligan Paul Minear L. Morris E. S. Fiorenza H. B. Swete		G. E. Ladd J. D. Pentecost J. Phillips Merrill C. Tenney Robert L. Thomas John Walvoord

Obviously, the four systems cannot all be right in the same place in the same way. Neither a majority vote nor a minority appeal produces adequate warrant for a belief in any one of the four. Instead, we must turn now to the difficulties within the systems and analyze to what extent each is capable of grappling with and addressing the concerns of its critics.

revision as time passed and, ultimately, to obscurity. . . . Moreover, the lack of consensus among interpreters as to the identification of historical details that supposedly fulfill the prophecies of the Apocalypse contributed to the school's demise" ("Introduction to Revelation," in *Four Views on the Book of Revelation*, 18).

Difficulties with the Interpretive Systems

The early part of this section focuses mainly on widespread difficulties—those that apply to several systems—rather than isolating the weaknesses of each system individually. Difficulties that are unique to each system will appear only at the end of the section.

Unwarranted Assumptions

Interpreters sometimes build upon unfounded assumptions in developing their positions. Although we all consider ourselves to be rational and consistent thinkers, and of course we strive to draw proper conclusions, unwarranted conclusions still exist.[15] A warranted conclusion has clear evidence *and* a clear connection with the evidence that backs it. An unwarranted conclusion lacks either the evidence, an adequate connection with the evidence, or both. Several assumptions that interpreters make concerning Revelation lack adequate warrant.

First, many interpreters make unwarranted genre assumptions. For instance, many interpreters assume that Revelation is an apocalypse. Appendix 1 demonstrates that this assessment is problematic on multiple grounds.[16] Recent preterist and idealist interpreters uniformly subscribe to the Revelation-as-apocalypse view. Some futurists, especially those who hold to progressive dispensationalism, concur. Compounding the previous problem is the assumption that a scriptural apocalypse (if it even exists) should

---

[15] The absence of warrant does not *make* something false. It simply breaks down the reasonable connection between the evidence and the conclusion. For example, I may claim that Mr. Smith stole my computer. When asked why I think he stole it, I could reply, "Just look at him. He's dirty and mean." My reason for believing that he stole my computer is inadequate. It lacks warrant. But Mr. Smith could be guilty, and his guilt could be established on warranted grounds such as his fingerprints all over my office, his possession of lock-picking tools, and his recent acquisition of money from a pawn shop known for dealing in computers.

[16] See "The Genre Argument—Revelation as Apocalypse" in appendix 1.

be treated with the same interpretive method as a fictional Jewish apocalypse.[17] Scripture itself provides no ground for interpreting Revelation differently from other books of the Bible.

Second, interpreters often insist on a symbolic or figurative interpretation without sufficient justification. Symbols occur periodically in Scripture, but the rampant assigning of symbolic meaning to prophecy finds no basis in grammatical-historical exegesis. Some interpreters assume that the images in Revelation are too fantastic to be literal. The slaying of 185,000 Assyrians in one night by one angel seems too fantastic to be literal, but the Old Testament assures us that such an event occurred. A virgin's bearing a child clearly stretches the bounds of reason, and a good symbolic interpreter in Isaiah's day could have found any number of reasons to explain the event away, but it occurred in the birth of Christ. Other interpreters assume that the presence of a few identified symbols in Revelation makes the entire book symbolic, but this assumption is both biblically and logically flawed. It is biblically flawed because many of the Old Testament prophets used symbolism at points (Jer. 1:11–16; Ezek. 37:1–14; Zech. 4:1–14) where not their entire books were symbolic. It is logically flawed because the fact that one green vegetable is a cucumber hardly makes all other green vegetables cucumbers, even if they came from the same garden.[18] Although its validity is conceivable,

---

[17] For example, see C. Marvin Pate and Calvin B. Haines Jr., *Doomsday Delusions: What's Wrong With Predictions About the End of the World* (Downers Grove: InterVarsity Press, 1995), 27, in which the writers argue that "the proper relationship between [literal and symbolic] is best accounted for by *beginning* with the figurative meaning." This statement follows a series of pages in which the writers insist on treating Revelation like a Jewish apocalypse.

[18] The fallacy is as follows: Some images in the prophetic books are symbolic. X is an image in a prophetic book. Therefore, X is symbolic. This makes as much sense as saying: Some male animals are human. My dog, Floppy, is male. Therefore, Floppy is human.

symbolic interpretation of Revelation as an interpretive axiom still awaits a convincing warrant.

Third, interpreters sometimes define a word in a way that is calculated to support their case even when that definition is tenuous.[19] For instance, one writer asserts, "Greek lexicons and modern translations agree that these terms ["soon" and "near"] indicate temporal proximity."[20] The writer apparently overlooks the fact that temporal manner (rapidity) is a more frequent use of the first Greek term in both the Septuagint and the New Testament, and it fits the context of Revelation as well.[21] Therefore we must be careful to select the best contextual meaning of individual words.

Fourth, envisioning a solution does not necessarily prove the validity of an interpretation. Our solution may indicate our creativity and imagination more than it indicates our accuracy of interpretation. For example, preterists in particular but also some historicists and idealists have taken the first beast to be a reference to Nero and the number 666 (or 616) as proof.[22] In order to make this work, the interpreter must take Nero's name from Latin, through Greek (Nέρων), into Hebrew (נרון). He then needs to add a title (Caesar; Καίσαρ) and to use defective spelling for Caesar (קסר in place of קיסר), and voila! Nero equals 666. Revelation indicates

[19] Stanley D. Toussaint, "A Critique of the Preterist View of the Olivet Discourse," *Bibliotheca Sacra* 161 (October–December 2004): 469–90, provides multiple examples of this abuse of individual terms. He demonstrates how the selection of a non-New Testament use of the words *parousia* (παρουσία) (476) and *all flesh* (πᾶσα σάρξ) (481) contributes to a preterist misinterpretation of the Olivet Discourse.

[20] Gentry, "A Preterist View," 41.

[21] A third meaning for this word also exists which fits both the immediate and the biblical context most clearly. This discussion will appear below under "Defense of Futurism, The 'Soon-' and 'Near-'ness of Revelation."

[22] See Mark L. Hitchcock, "A Critique of the Preterist View of Revelation 13 and Nero," *Bibliotheca Sacra* 164 (2007): 341–56, for a discussion of the number 666 and its attendant difficulties.

that 666 is the number of the beast's name, however, not of his title. Once the interpreter allows (1) the addition of any and all titles that could be associated with a figure, (2) transliteration (with all its attendant difficulties) into any language required to make the identification work, and (3) any spelling necessary to make the interpretation work, he cuts himself off from any warranted confidence in the accuracy of his interpretation.[23] Virtually any name will work.[24]

Loss of Interpretive Control

Preterism, Historicism, and Idealism replace literal with symbolic interpretation. This exchange cuts the book off from a grammatical-historical mooring and leads to a loss of interpretive control by the text. The imagination of the interpreter replaces the original author's meaning even where the interpreter tries to exercise caution in his use of symbolism.[25] This loss of interpretive control tends toward a loss of certainty concerning the book's message. As soon

[23] G. Salmon observes, "We cannot infer much from the fact that a key fits the lock if it is a lock in which almost any key will turn." *An Historical Introduction to the Study of the Books of the New Testament*, 9th ed. (London: John Murray, 1904), 230–31.

[24] Kenneth L. Gentry Jr. makes a startling admission against interest in regard to the interpretation of 666 when he writes, "It would seem most reasonable to expect that since Irenaeus wrote within about one hundred years of Revelation, he likely would have heard of the proper view. At the very least, we would think, Irenaeus would recognize the true view, though growing indistinct, as a theory to be given equal footing with the solutions he does proffer. But, as a matter of fact, in his lengthy treatment of the gematria in *Against Heresies* 5:28–30 (especially chapter 30), he provides at least three possible interpretations—and Nero's name is conspicuously absent. Furthermore, *no* early Church father suggests Nero's name as the proper designation of 666, even though various suggestions were given by such men as Irenaeus, Andreas of Caesarea, Victorinus, Hippolytus, Clement of Alexandria, and others." *Before Jerusalem Fell: Dating the Book of Revelation*, rev. ed. (Atlanta: American Vision, 1998), 205.

[25] Many symbolic interpreters try to outline procedures by which a symbol should be interpreted, but rarely can they follow their own procedures consistently. Imagination runs too freely to be bridled easily. Mark L. Hitchcock documents several examples of this inconsistency in "A Critique of the Preterist View of the Temple in Revelation 11:1–2," *Bibliotheca Sacra* 164 (2007): 225.

as the text enters the realm of the symbolic, the interpreter (and his followers or readers) cannot be sure of the validity of his interpretation.[26] He is only as certain as his imagination has convinced him to be. In this condition, no interpretation or interpreter has greater claim to authority than any other, as long as it (or he) remains within general doctrinal confines.

Evidence of the loss of interpretive control appears in the wildly vacillating application of interpretive methods. For example, although Preterism interprets virtually everything else in the book of Revelation figuratively, it takes the "soon" reference of 1:1 literally (and narrowly). Many idealists interpret the entire book as having no referent to reality other than on the level of general principle until they come to the Second Coming of Christ. They take this isolated event literally and then return to symbolic interpretation for their understanding of the New Jerusalem and the eternal state. No system has successfully provided a foundational warrant for abandoning the literal interpretation of Scripture in the first place, and neither Preterism nor Idealism can warrant its individual interpretive shifts from the context.

Loss of Meaning

As soon as the text loses its control over the reader, it also loses its ability to communicate its meaning consistently and coherently. We see this problem unfolding in the reader-response theories of twentieth-century literary criticism. Each reader creates his own meaning, and the meaning intended by the author evaporates. This is one of the great defects in Idealism. It eviscerates the

[26] Commentators, especially those of the preterist, idealist, and historicist positions, concur that the "key" to interpreting Revelation has been lost. See Tenney, 186. If the key is lost, our investigation amounts to speculation. At the very least our certainty concerning correct interpretation diminishes significantly.

majestic Christology and poignant eschatology of Revelation and replaces both with a bland, though true, principle: good wins, evil loses. Idealism reflects general truth, but it damages the communication of the *full* truth by truncating biblical reality. The loss of information would correspond to the loss we would incur if someone treated the book of Romans symbolically and turned it into this three-fold proclamation: man is bad; Jesus saves; trust Jesus. All of the statements are true. All of them appear in Romans. But the summary does not do justice to the themes and message of Romans. If the images of Revelation do not connect to real time and space, the best that we can glean from them is an emotional impression of victory. We cannot study the connections between words, phrases, sentences, and sections with any definitive spiritual profit. This reductionist perspective requires too high a price, especially when the text does not provide an adequate warrant for the interpretive choice.[27]

System Incoherence

Preterism, Historicism, and Idealism do not offer the interpreter a coherent, consistent system.[28] This fact does not trouble the proponents of these systems overmuch since disjointed apocalyptic visions and symbolic images require no coherence or consistency. Although each of these interpretive positions explains isolated

[27] "Too high a price" is a value judgment, but Scripture warrants it. The prophet in the Old Testament was vindicated by the fulfillment of his prophecy. Where prophecy is so vague or general as to approach meaninglessness, "fulfillment" cannot vindicate the prophet. In fact, pagan deities, including the Delphic Oracle, gave exactly the kind of "prophecies" that Idealism expects from Revelation. According to legend, King Croesus of Lydia asked the oracle if he should attack the Persians. He received the answer, "If you cross the river, a great empire will be destroyed." He crossed the river and was destroyed by the Persians. The Old Testament demonstrates that God proves Himself by means of His exact, specific, revealed knowledge of the future (Isa. 42:8–9; 46:9–11; 48:3–8).

[28] I do not intend this statement to be abusive of these interpreters or an *ad hominem* attack. Rather, I simply acknowledge what most of them acknowledge: we could drop the word *system* from Preterism, Historicism, and Idealism and replace it with *hermeneutic*.

passages, they do not address grammar in a consistent fashion nor systematize the prophetic passages of Scripture adequately.

For example, one writer thinks he has vindicated Preterism by insisting that since we presently rule with Christ in His kingdom, Revelation 20 cannot refer to a future event and must refer to the past.[29] But at what point do believers start to reign with Christ? At the destruction of Jerusalem? No. Since Gentry refers to Ephesians 2:6 as warrant for his position, even by his standards we would have to start our reign at the point of salvation. John clearly predicts our reign with Christ as future (Rev. 20:6). If John wrote ca. AD 66–68, how can the reign of believers be construed as future from his vantage point when it has already been going on for over thirty-five years? Paul says we are seated with Christ in heavenly places already. John says this reign is still future. John wrote after Paul; therefore, John and Paul cannot be referring to the same thing. None of the verses Gentry cites demonstrate a present reign of believers at all. Second Timothy 2:12 and Revelation 5:10 and 20:6 concur that our reign is still future. Preterism misinterprets passages in Paul and then applies that misinterpretation to Revelation in the attempt to prove the system. In the process Preterism creates an incoherent "system."[30]

The interpretation of "the beast" offered by Preterism calls the prophetic capacity of John into question. For example, claiming that Nero is the beast in view in Revelation 13 and 17 makes Revelation false prophecy. Although a certain attractive link exists between the *Nero redivivus* myth of the first century and the

---

[29] Gentry, "A Preterist View," 85.

[30] Examples could be multiplied almost endlessly, but this work seeks to advocate a proper approach to the interpretation of Revelation more than it seeks to redress the problems created by poor interpretation.

prophecy of Revelation 13:3 and 17:10, the interpreters who follow this interpretation turn Revelation 17:8 into nonsense. That verse explicitly indicates that the beast (1) was, (2) is not, and (3) is about to come up from the abyss. Even 13:3 indicates that the beast suffered a (nearly?) fatal head wound and yet lived. Moreover, people see him visibly alive. According to Revelation 17:8, there was no *myth* about the beast's re-living and returning to power. The beast must live again! Either Nero rose visibly from the dead, returned to control over the entire Roman Empire in greater fashion than ever before, and was involved in the destruction of Jerusalem (none of which happened), or John was a false prophet, or Preterism misinterprets the events of Revelation. The final option is the only viable one.

Historicism fails to produce coherence since it offers no secure method of matching images with events. Having removed literal interpretation from its position of authority, Historicism has failed to replace it with a clear alternative. No clear time interval exists between a symbol and its referent or between one referent and another. No consistent degree of specificity exists between an image and its referent. Only the intensity of the interpreter's imagination bridles the outcome of the historicist's method.

Idealism cannot present a coherent interpretation of Revelation because it offers essentially an anti-system rather than a system. It denies literal referents, turns specifics into generalities, and thereby excuses itself from having to explain when, where, and how these events occur. These reductionist (or even deconstructionist) tendencies cannot produce a coherent explanation of the expectations and events in any of the prophetic books of Scripture. At least Preterism and Historicism grapple with the interpretive issues seriously. Idealism sweeps all interpretive clarity away with its generic symbolism. If Scripture explicitly warranted such treatment, we certainly could not complain, but the futurist protests that the Bible nowhere urges or countenances the use of an interpretive method that reduces order and specific persons and events to a jumbled mix of subjective impressions. Idealism offers interpretive anarchy in place of coherence.

Additional Weaknesses of Preterism

Preterism is more directly refutable than Idealism since Preterism commits itself to actual exegesis of passages. Where poor exegesis occurs, we can assess and reject it. The following weaknesses appear in the preterist system and undermine its credibility.

A late date for Revelation threatens the entire preterist system. If John wrote in the reign of Domitian, the events of Revelation could not pertain to the destruction of Jerusalem, but the evidence from the early church points to just such a late date.[31] Preterism rejects the testimony of the early church as mistaken, but this rejection rests more on the necessity of such a rejection for the system than on actual evidence. The majority of scholars recognize the strength of early church testimony and accept the late date.

The early church fathers do not look back on the destruction of Jerusalem as the *parousia* (coming of Christ in judgment). Had Jesus' teaching been so clear that He was coming soon in judgment,

---

[31] Non-preterists consider this to be the death-knell of the entire system. The fact that the early witness of the church points uniformly to the late date seriously undermines preterist claims. Richard L. Mayhue, "Jesus: A Preterist or a Futurist?" *The Master's Seminary Journal* 14, no. 1 (Spring 2003): 13–14. Mayhue also observes that the proper setting of the church conditions in Revelation 2–3 occurred in the 90s rather than in the 60s. Even secular sociologists concur that "the best analysis of pagan and Christian sources suggests that Revelation was indeed written toward the end of Domitian's reign." David A. deSilva, "The Revelation to John: A Case Study in Apocalyptic Propaganda and the Maintenance of Sectarian Identity," *Sociological Analysis* 53, no. 4 (Winter 1992): 377.

the early church could not have failed to interpret Revelation from the preterist perspective, but the early church was premillennial (futurist).

Preterism relies heavily on its particular exegesis of difficult passages. It insists, for example, that Matthew 10:23 indicates a soon coming of Christ since the disciples would not even finish going through the cities of Israel before the Son of Man would come. But this passage actually says, "You shall by no means finish the cities of Israel until the Son of Man should come." "Going through" is not part of the text. "Finishing your witness in," "evangelizing," or even "converting" are just as viable as options, and all of these correspond better with other Scriptures such as Romans 11:25–32. Preterism next relies on Matthew 16:28 to establish its system. It asserts that Christ's coming in His kingdom must mean His judgment on Jerusalem. This interpretation causes problems since the phrase "the Son of man coming in his kingdom" has at least six possible interpretations, only one of which could support Preterism. Better interpretations of Matthew 16:28 take Christ's coming in His kingdom at His Transfiguration (proleptically of His glory at His second coming) or at Pentecost (when the coming of the Holy Spirit indicated Christ's session at the right hand of the Father).

Preterism assigns unnatural meaning to technical terms and can base its decision for the unnatural usage only on the passages in question.[32] For example, the New Testament uses *parousia* to refer to an actual, bodily presence rather than to the preterists' idea of a spiritual presence.[33] This is true even in Matthew 24, where the

---

[32] Mark L. Hitchcock shows how Gentry narrows the expression "all the tribes of the earth" to Jews in Judea in spite of the fact that all the Septuagint occurrences of that expression refer to humanity universally. "A Critique of the Preterist View of Revelation and the Jewish War," *Bibliotheca Sacra* 164 (2007): 92.

[33] Toussaint, 476.

word appears four times (vv. 3, 27, 37, 39). Only the instance in verse 27 is really in question. The disciples were asking concerning the actual, bodily return of Christ (v. 3), and even many preterists admit that verse 36 shifts to the future when it moves from "this generation" (v. 34) to "that day."

Preterism relies on terms for the "soon"-ness and "near"-ness of Revelation (1:1, 3; 22:6, 10)[34] to argue that the events portrayed in the book must happen soon with reference to John's prophecy. This argument does not actually solve the problem for Preterism, though. Mark Hitchcock observes, "With these statements serving as bookends for the entire prophetic content of Revelation, whatever meaning one gives to these terms must be applied to all the events in the book."[35] This means that the Second Coming of Christ, the resurrection of the dead, the final rebellion of Satan, the final judgment of the Great White Throne, and the creation of the new heavens and new earth had to have happened in the same time period, at the destruction of Jerusalem. The argument that moderate Preterism uses to establish its system vitiates its system. If moderate Preterism applies its interpretation of "soon" and "near" consistently, it must become radical Preterism, which is heretical.[36]

---

[34] See the section on "The 'Soon-' and 'Near-'ness of Revelation" below.

[35] Mark L. Hitchcock, "A Critique of the Preterist View of 'Soon' and 'Near' in Revelation," *Bibliotheca Sacra* 163 (2006): 472. Consistent preterist John Noē agrees with Hitchcock's assessment: "Preterists argue that these full context-embracing phrases demand fulfillment of the whole prophecy within a very short time and certainly within the lifetime of the book's original recipients. This includes the consummation and glorious coming/return of Christ in finality." "An Exegetical Basis for a Preterist-Idealist Understanding of the Book of Revelation," *Journal of the Evangelical Theological Society* 49, no. 4 (December 2006): 770. In his article Noē offers four syllogisms to prove Preterism. Three of the four exhibit the fallacy of the shared characteristic and *non sequitur* reasoning.

[36] Hitchcock also observes, "A consistent interpretation of these timing terms demands either a futurist or a full preterist approach to Revelation. And since full or radical Preterism denies a literal second coming of Christ and the future bodily resurrection, this

No historical figure during the time of Nero meets the qualifications for "second beast" status.[37] The false prophet of Revelation sides with the beast (13:12), causes humanity to worship the beast (13:12), does miracles (13:13), gives life to the image of the beast (13:15), and causes mankind to take the mark of the beast (13:16). No one did these things in the first century. Preterism's assessment of the events of Revelation does not withstand the scrutiny of careful observation and exegesis.

Additional Weakness of Historicism

The inability of interpreters to attach the images of Revelation consistently to historical events constitutes probably the most decisive rebuttal of Historicism. Since nothing in Revelation matches the invasions of the Goths, the raids of Attila the Hun, the Muslim assault on Vienna, or the rise of Adolf Hitler, historicists must apply images arbitrarily. This leads to substantial disagreement among proponents of the system. Each new generation of historicists stretches the timeline a little further in order to reassess that generation's place on the timeline of history. Historicism does not warrant our confidence.

Additional Weakness of Idealism

Idealism desires to find an immediate application for the church in the book of Revelation. This desire springs from a correct recognition that no part of Scripture fails to accomplish its divinely ordained work in the lives of God's people. A difficulty arises,

view is outside the pale of orthodoxy" ("A Critique of the Preterist View of 'Soon' and 'Near,'" 472).

[37] Hitchcock observes that although Gentry makes a weak attempt to identify the second beast as Gessius Florus, a Roman-Jewish procurator over Judea under Nero, Gentry offers absolutely no historical evidence to support the claim ("A Critique of the Preterist View of Revelation 13 and Nero," 353–54). Gessius Florus did nothing even remotely approximating the power and signs of the second beast.

however, when Idealism replaces meaning with application. A proper method of interpretation strives to discern the meaning of the text for its original audience. This does not imply that everything in a given text occurred in the time of the original audience, but that the text meant something in particular as it came from the author. Application stems from meaning. For example, as we examine what the Mosaic law meant for Israel, we do not conclude that the Mosaic law holds authority over us in the church today. We would be misinterpreting the Old Testament if we concluded that since the Mosaic law as written holds no obvious and direct "meaning" for us today, the entire legal code is symbolic. We cannot look for application at the expense of meaning.

In Revelation, Idealism searches so diligently for relevant application throughout the church age that it insists the book must be symbolic. Idealists contend that unless Revelation operates on the spiritual level, it cannot apply to the church today and is entirely worthless. On the contrary, futurists insist that its meaning underlies all genuine application. The fact that these events will occur literally in the future may make application to the present more difficult for the interpreter, but the difficulty does not warrant his choosing the easier path of spiritualization. To be fair, the idealist would argue that he is pursuing the original meaning. He just happens to believe that the original meaning was entirely symbolic. That interpretive position cuts Revelation loose from actual interpretation, however, since we have already noted that if the book is (almost) entirely symbolic, and the key is lost (and it most certainly is lost), then nothing constrains the imagination of the individual interpreter. This results in a situation, intended or not, in which application is the deciding factor in interpretation. Conservative idealists will use conservative doctrine derived from the rest of Scripture to find conservative applications in Revelation, but their application has overridden exegesis.

Summary

Taken individually, these difficulties do not overwhelm a particular interpretive position, but their aggregate weight inclines many interpreters toward a more consistent solution.

Defense of Futurism

The case for a futurist interpretation of Revelation proceeds both positively and negatively. Positively, the evidence from natural interpretation, continuity with the Old Testament, and coherence as a system argue in favor of futurism as the best method of interpretation. Negatively, futurism has the capacity to answer the charges of its critics.

Positive Case

Futurism is not an anti-system. It does not rely exclusively on the refutation of other systems in order to ground its case. Instead, several lines of evidence warrant confidence in Futurism as the most natural explanation of the events in Revelation.

Natural Hermeneutics

Conservatives agree that the interpretation of Scripture must follow the grammatical-historical method.[38] This method consists of literal interpretation. The grammatical-historical method led the Reformers out of the Roman Catholic Church and brought them to understand justification by faith. It exposed Rome's interpretation of Scripture and its defense of papal authority as exegetically and theologically bankrupt. Commentators recognize the

[38] See Terry, 203–10.

grammatical-historical method to be the foundation of all solid exegesis and exposition. One of the basic rules of grammatical-historical exegesis is the insistence on the literal meaning unless the context clearly requires otherwise.[39]

Many writers confuse the literal *method* (or literal *interpretation*) with the literal *meaning* of a given word or phrase. If a writer merges these two ideas, he can create a straw man that is easily dismissed as untrue to normal communication. For example, when the preterist or idealist picks out an isolated, indisputably figurative image in Revelation and scoffs at the literal interpreter for his presumed inability to fit the image into his system without spiritualizing it, he uses the logical fallacy of the straw man argument.

The literal *method* recognizes that unless the context clearly indicates otherwise, the interpreter must take a given word, phrase, or image literally. When a given word, phrase, or image has a literal *meaning*, this indicates the opposite of its being figurative. Futurists do not deny that Revelation uses figures of speech and even symbolism. They do not insist on a literal meaning for everything in the book. They deny that the book requires a symbolic *method* of interpretation that Preterism, Historicism, and Idealism require. Applying a symbolic method to Scripture is simply poor hermeneutics.

Many of the same interpreters who defend grammatical-historical exegesis in the rest of Scripture reject the predominantly literal interpretation of biblical prophecy. But the careful study of biblical prophecy—both that which was fulfilled in the Old Testament and that which relates to Jesus' first coming—leaves the reader with the unmistakable impression that prophecy, too, is *predominantly*

[39] "The grammatical sense is essentially the same as the literal" (Terry, 203).

literal. Many writers have observed this fact. J. D. Pentecost has said, "Without doubt the greatest confirmation of the literal method of interpreting prophecies comes from an observation of the method God has employed to fulfill the prophecies that have already been fulfilled."[40] Table 3 in chapter 1 provided a few examples of this phenomenon.

Although some interpreters circumvent the force of this argument by appealing to Old Testament prophecies against Babylon that have not been fulfilled literally, these interpreters assume that Babylon has no more place in God's plan for the future. But this is precisely one of the points in question.[41] Futurism argues that Babylon does have a place in eschatology and that the Old Testament prophecies concerning Babylon will receive a predominantly literal fulfillment.[42] A natural response to this futurist argument would be that the futurist position cannot be falsified since it can always remove to a distant time period any prophecies that have not been fulfilled literally. In some sense this concern is well founded. Futurism does seem to insulate itself from critique by appealing to distant, unverifiable events, but this observation does not warrant the conclusion that Futurism lacks interpretive merit,

---

[40] J. Dwight Pentecost, *Things to Come: A Study in Biblical Eschatology* (Grand Rapids: Zondervan, 1958), 60.

[41] Babylon could rise again. See Eduard Gismatullin, "Rebuilding Babylon," *The Moscow Times*, November 20, 1999; and Jeffrey Gettleman, "Ruined Treasures in Babylon Await an Iraq Without Fighting," *The New York Times*, April 18, 2006.

[42] A "predominantly literal" interpretation allows for figures of speech where they occur. For example, when Isaiah 40:3 calls for the people to "prepare . . . the way of the Lord, make straight in the desert a highway for our God," Isaiah does not expect road construction crews to jump into action. In the ancient world, a city or region that expected a great king to pass through its territory would smooth the roads, minimize the bumps, and generally "pave the way" for him to pass. This is what the text indicates. It is interesting that even in English we have a figurative expression for the same idea: "pave the way." Futurists admit such figures of speech. They have no antipathy toward figures and symbols that corresponds to the antipathy of Preterism, Historicism, and Idealism toward the literal.

especially when the natural grammatical-historical method is the default for all normal communication and for conservative interpretation.[43] Attempting to shift the burden of proof onto Futurism does not obviate the extreme difficulty that fulfilled prophecy produces for Preterism, Historicism, and Idealism.

As long as the Bible uses "fulfillment" terminology fairly consistently to describe predominantly literal outcomes to earlier prophecies, exegesis *ought* to conclude that prophecy receives a predominantly literal fulfillment. On this point the futurist stakes his case. From clearly stated biblical examples, where prophecy is fulfilled, it is fulfilled in a predominantly literal fashion. A figurative fulfillment is the exception, not the rule. Thus the grammatical-historical interpreter should expect the literal while admitting the possibility of the figurative, not the other way around. And as Robert L. Thomas observes, "The futurist approach to the book is the only view that grants sufficient recognition to the prophetic style of the book and a normal hermeneutical pattern of interpretation based on that style."[44]

Futurism insists that the burden of proof remain on those who would depart from normal interpretation in a given passage. It does not insist that every image receive a pedantically literal interpretation. Where Futurism departs from the literal, it must provide a clear warrant for the departure, and it insists that other systems do the same.

---

[43] See the "Response to Criticism" section below.

[44] Robert L. Thomas, "Literary Genre and Hermeneutics of the Apocalypse," in *The Master's Perspective on Biblical Prophecy*, ed. Richard L. Mayhue and Robert L. Thomas, vol. 4. of The Master's Perspective Series (Grand Rapids: Kregel Publications, 2002), 100.

Continuity with Old Testament Prophecies and Expectations

A natural interpretation of the book of Revelation corroborates rather than undermines Old Testament prophetic expectations, especially with reference to Israel.[45] Old Testament prophecy indicates unequivocally that Israel should expect, among other events, (1) Messiah's setting up a physical, earthly kingdom while reigning on the throne of David, (2) Israel's rise to worldwide prominence, and (3) a final and irrevocable defeat of Israel's perennial and eschatological enemies. These expectations offer such a decisive theological position and eschatological hope that even opponents of literal interpretation admit the tenor and direction of the thrust of Old Testament prophecy.[46] Herman Bavinck, observes:

> These messianic expectations of the Old Testament, as any reader can see at once, are of a unique kind: they limit themselves to a future blessed state *on earth*. . . . As a rule, the eye of prophecy is directed toward that future in which the people of Israel will live securely under a king of David's dynasty in Palestine and will rule over all the nations of the earth.[47]

[45] A link does exist between Futurism and other belief systems. Those who have dismissed the promises God made to Israel by spiritualizing them and folding them into the church rarely hold a futurist perspective. Dispensationalists hold uniformly to Futurism. Covenant premillennialists also accept Futurism. Most covenant theologians subscribe to replacement theology, in which the church has replaced Israel in God's plan. Those who hold to this view tend strongly toward Idealism or Preterism.

[46] John. F. Walvoord corroborates this assertion when he notes, "If the Old Testament is interpreted literally in its prophetic anticipation, it leads directly to the concept that when Christ returns, He will bring in His kingdom on earth. Even scholars of other persuasions often admit that such is the case. Not only do they concede that the Old Testament interpreted literally yields such a doctrine but clearly recognize that the people of Israel anticipated such a Messiah and such a kingdom" (*Prophecy*, 137).

[47] Herman Bavinck, *The Last Things: Hope for This World and the Next*, ed. John Bolt, trans. John Vriend (Grand Rapids: Baker Books, 1996), 89. After recognizing the clear statements and implications of the Old Testament prophecies, Bavinck proceeds to explain these away by claiming that Israel's prophets had to put future events in terms of the present. Since Israel's prophets could not foresee the spiritual application of their

Table 5 depicts visually how a futurist view of Revelation coincides with these Old Testament prophecies and broadly Jewish expectations.

Table 5—Continuity of Futurism & OT Expectations

Expectation	OT Prophecy	Revelation
Israel rises to worldwide prominence	Joel 3:17, 20 Amos 9:11 Zeph. 3:20	7:4–8
Israel's temple rebuilt	Joel 3:18 Zech. 14:20	11:1–2
Israel goes through severe tribulation	Amos 9:9 Zech. 14:2	12:13, 15
Israel's enemies experience a final and irrevocable defeat	Joel 3:9–17 Mic. 5:9 Zeph. 3:15–18 Zech. 12, 14	14:8; 16:19; 18:1–24; 19:11–21
Messiah on earthly throne of David and Israel	Isa. 9:6–7 Amos 9:11 Mic. 5:2, 4	20:4

Coherence as a System

Futurism offers a thoroughly developed system that takes both Old and New Testament prophecy seriously and literally.[48] It does not

prophecies, they had to communicate in earthly, Israel-centered terms (90). Finally, he rejects literal interpretation altogether (95) and later claims that "the chiliastic expectation that a converted nation of Israel, restored to the land of Palestine, under Christ will rule over the nations is without biblical foundation" (99). His comments are inherently self-contradictory. After he admits that all the Old Testament prophets predicted, longed for, and understood a literal, physical, earthly kingdom of Messiah, to claim that such a kingdom is "without biblical foundation" is a perfect example of one's theological tradition overriding clear biblical claims.

[48] Gary G. Cohen provides repeated documentation of how Revelation coincides with the time references in Daniel, how it fits the Scripture-wide scope of data on eschatology, and how it provides an internally consistent depiction of time. *Understanding Revelation: A Chronology of the Apocalypse* (Collingswood, NJ: Christian Beacon Press, 1968). Cohen states, "The Futuristic approach to the Apocalypse is the only one (*contra*—Liberal;

need to explain every detail of the future or be capable of integrating every prophecy into some sort of artificial equation in order to be valid. No human understands the counsels of God enough to accomplish that level of precision, but Futurism avoids the internal incoherence that is commonplace in the other systems.[49]

Some of the most regularly cited "inconsistencies" in Futurism actually prove the point. When Idealism and Preterism claim that Futurism skews the imagery of Revelation by separating the events of the seventh trumpet and bowl into different time frames, they fail to recognize two crucial facts. First, lightning, thunder, and earthquakes are fairly common events in association with the divine presence and divine judgment (Exod. 9:23–34; 19:16; 1 Sam. 7:10; 12:17–18; Ps. 77:18).[50] These are literal events repeated in Scripture. Second, many futurists accept a telescopic view of Revelation's structure, which would envelop the bowl judgments in the seventh trumpet, allowing the seventh of both to occur at

---

Allegorical; Preterit; Historical; & Topical) which harmonizes Daniel (9:24, 26–27; 7:19–27; 8:23–25); Matthew (24 and 25—esp. 24:15–23, 29–31); 2 Thess. (2:1–12); Jer. 30:4–10; Rom. 11:25–26; Jn. 5:23; Zech. 12:9–14; 8:23; Jer. 23:5–8; *et cetera* into one unified eschatological program" (41).

[49] G. K. Beale's assessment that Rev. 12:7–11 and Rev. 20:1–6 are the same event illustrates the contradictions that Idealism faces and simply dismisses (992). He says both begin with a "heavenly scene." But Rev. 12 is war in heaven, and Rev. 20 is war on earth (the angel comes down from heaven and *then* lays hold of Satan). The passage forces Idealism to insert a "presupposed angelic battle with Satan" in ch. 20 where none is found. Ch. 12 sends Satan to the earth. Ch. 20 sends him *from* the earth into the abyss. In ch. 12 Satan is operationally deceiving the nations, while in ch. 20 he is prevented from deceiving the nations. If language really is this flexible and ambiguous, then Revelation teaches nothing coherent, since all time, space, order, and events have absolutely no grounding in reality, and conflicting statements can be made to attest one in the same event.

[50] While the lightning, thunder, and earthquakes in the book of Revelation certainly do not reduce to merely natural instances of these phenomena, the fact that they recur in chs. 6, 11, and 16 hardly warrants a recapitulatory interpretation for the book as a whole. Several million earthquakes occur worldwide each year. As many as eight million lightning strikes occur daily in the world. And we have no means of calculating how often or for what purpose these events occur in heaven.

the same time. This is not the type of problem that Idealism and Preterism face when they try to make the seals, trumpets, and bowls recapitulate each other and end up with directly contradictory statements, such as silence (8:1) occurring at the same time and in the same place as loud voices (11:15), and men hiding from God in the mountains (6:15–16) while openly and brazenly gathering together to fight God in the field (16:14–16). Idealists and preterists try to solve the problem by removing all order from the seals, trumpets, and bowls so that recapitulation does not actually have to recapitulate in any defined order, place, or event, but this is precisely the difference in systems. Futurism coheres. The other systems "incohere"; that is, they must fracture, fragment, rearrange, and reinterpret every event and image in order to make sense of them.

Statement of Purpose

Revelation opens with a statement of purpose: "The revelation of Jesus Christ, which God gave him to show to his servants the things that must soon take place." This statement explicitly indicates that God intends for Revelation to reveal the future. Although the book may comfort believers, that comfort is an effect or an application of God's purpose. Although it may corroborate the general struggle between good and evil, that corroboration is incidental to its purpose. Revelation reveals the future. Thus the stated purpose of Revelation coincides best with the futurist interpretation of the book.

Response to Criticism

The "Soon-" and "Near-"ness of Revelation

One of the strongest critiques of Futurism rests on the interpretation of several words near the opening and closing of Revelation. Table 6 charts the occurrences of these words in Revelation. If the words must mean "soon" in the sense of temporal proximity, Futurism faces the dilemma of explaining away the text or ignoring it altogether. Preterism argues for the "soon-ness" of Revelation most vehemently, and Historicism claims that its events *begin* to take place "soon." Idealism garbles the reference entirely, since there is no specific fulfillment of the images of Revelation anywhere in history. Futurism rejects the claim that the events took place within a temporally immediate time frame after John wrote.

On the other hand, only those Preterists who (1) believe in an early date for the book and (2) see the *entire* book fulfilled in the destruction of Jerusalem actually solve the problem, since Revelation does not indicate that the events will merely *start* to take place in the near future. Most Preterists, those who are actually more consistent with handling the data on the intersection of a world empire and persecuted Christians, see some of the book's fulfillment in the downfall of Rome, more than four hundred years distant. Obviously, this belief places serious strains on their credibility when they attack futurists for believing the events are over nineteen hundred years in the future.

TABLE 6—TEMPORAL SETTING OF THE BOOK OF REVELATION

Reference	Greek Term	Translation
1:1	τάχος	to shew unto his servants things which must shortly come to pass
1:3	ἐγγύς	for the time *is* at hand
22:6	τάχος	to shew unto his servants the things which must shortly be done
22:7	ταχύς	behold, I come quickly
22:10	ἐγγύς	for the time is at hand

Reference	Greek Term	Translation
22:12	ταχύς	behold, I come quickly
22:20	ταχύς	surely I come quickly

The Meaning of "Soon" in Scripture

Theological systems often explain away data that is inconvenient for their views, but Futurism does not need to resort to unusual interpretive measures to deal with the inconvenience of the passages cited above. Instead, it urges the reader to examine the biblical contexts in which these words occur to see whether Scripture warrants a solution to the problem.

Four Greek words appear in Scripture with *tach-* as their stem.[51] *Tach-* related words most often mean "quickly," but they can also mean "soon" or "imminently." The most common use expresses chronological speed or manner (*how*), not chronological nearness or proximity (*when*). Examining these words in the prophetic books of the Bible (see table 7) shows us that "nearness" in time is rarely in view (with the occurrences in Revelation being the only claimed exceptions). On the other hand, the imminence of the event (both its any-time-ness and its certainty) stands out frequently as the natural meaning in context.

Table 7—*Tach-* in Prophetic Contexts

	ταχέως	ταχινός	τάχος	ταχύς
Swiftness	Joel 3:4 [4:4 LXX] Isa. 8:3 Dan. 2:16	Isa. 59:7 Hab. 1:6	Isa. 5:19 Dan. 9:21	Isa. 5:26 Isa. 32:4 Isa. 49:17 Jer. 49:19 [30:13 LXX]

[51] These are τάχος, ταχύς, ταχέως, and ταχινός. The adverb appears also in a comparative (τάχιον) and a superlative (τάχιστα) form.

	ταχέως	ταχινός	τάχος	ταχύς
Chronological Nearness Alone	None in prophetic contexts			
Imminence		2 Pet. 1:14[52] 2 Pet. 2:1[53]	Luke 18:8 Rom. 16:20	Isa. 9:1 [8:23 LXX] Isa. 13:22 Isa. 51:5 Jer. 48:16 [31:16 LXX] Zeph. 1:14 Mal. 3:5 Rev. 2:16 Rev. 3:11
Swiftness or Imminence	Jer. 50:44 [27:44 LXX]		Ezek. 29:5	Isa. 58:8 Nah. 1:14
Swiftness or Chronological Nearness				Rev. 11:14
Uses in Question			Rev. 1:1 Rev. 22:6	Rev. 22:7 Rev. 22:12 Rev. 22:20

When the futurist sees *imminence* in Revelation 1:1; 22:6, 7, 12, 20, he is not engaging in wishful thinking or speculative exegesis. Futurism relies on the actual usage of the Greek terms throughout biblical prophecy.

The Meaning of "Near" in Scripture

Proper analysis of Revelation requires the examination of a second term, however. Critics of Futurism use this term, appearing in Revelation 1:3 and 22:10, to dispute the data cited above. Surely

[52] W. Robertson Nicoll observes that the term means "imminent" in this location. *The Expositor's Greek Testament* (Grand Rapids: Eerdmans, 1961), 129.

[53] "'Swift' . . . here seems clearly to denote 'sudden,' although not necessarily 'soon.'" D. Edmond Hiebert, *Second Peter and Jude: An Expositional Commentary* (Greenville, SC: Unusual Publications, 1989), 91. "For a similar use of *tachinē*, 'sudden', used of Peter's own death, see 1:14." Michael Green, *2 Peter and Jude*, rev. ed. Tyndale New Testament Commentaries (Grand Rapids: Eerdmans, 1987), 106–07.

"near" can have no other meaning than temporal proximity. It is undeniable that ἐγγύς most frequently refers to an actual nearness of time or place, but once again the prophetic contexts lessen the one-sidedness of the evidence.

In Isaiah 13, God predicts the total desolation of the Babylonian empire. He specifies one agent of judgment in verse 17 as the Medes, and He indicates the extent of judgment in verse 20 as so thorough that Babylon would never again be inhabited. The Septuagint uses both of our crucial words to describe this destruction. Verse 22 uses "soon" (ταχύς) and verse 6 uses "near" or "at hand" (ἐγγύς). At this point the prophetic problem enters. Isaiah made this prophecy ca. 700 BC, when Babylon was not even a world power. Babylon rose to power and subjugated the Assyrians in 612 BC. The Medes overthrew Babylon in 539 BC. Thus God indicates that Babylon's overthrow will be "soon" and "near" 160 years before it happened. This evidence hardly fits the preterist and idealist insistence on temporal immediacy. The case gets even stronger, however, when we realize that Babylon's overthrow by the Medes was extremely mild in terms of the overthrow of empires. The Medes did not devastate the city. They did not plunder and murder the citizenry. They did not overthrow the economy, the governmental structures, or the physical buildings. In other words, the events of Isaiah 13 (and of Jeremiah 50–51) remain unfulfilled even today. God said these events were "soon" and "near," but at least twenty-seven hundred years have elapsed without their occurrence.[54]

The Naturalness of Imminency

The evidence that we possess from the earliest extant interpretations of Revelation indicates that the early church did not take the

[54] Hitchcock adds the fact that "the New Testament authors consistently describe this present age, or the time between the two comings, as the 'last days' or 'latter days.' In 1 John 2:18 the apostle even designated the present age as the 'last hour.' This means that

"soon-" and "near-"ness of Revelation to mean anything other than imminence. Recognizing how biblical prophecy operates, the early church did not view a gap in time as contradictory to the prophecy. On occasion, heresy arose when someone demanded an *immediate* fulfillment of prophecy (2 Tim. 2:17–18) in place of an imminent fulfillment. Taking "soon" and "near" to indicate imminence violates no linguistic rules, and the early church's handling of the matter adds credibility to the argument that imminence is a perfectly natural meaning of the Greek terms in Revelation 1:1 and 1:3.

An excellent illustration of imminence appears in Isaiah 30:13: "Therefore this iniquity shall be to you as a breach ready to fall, swelling out in a high wall, whose breaking cometh suddenly at an instant." An overhanging rock may sit immobile for hundreds of years, but make no mistake, it will eventually fall. It may fall today, a year from now, or a hundred years from now. We can't know the timing, but we can know its surety. This is the warning that the Old Testament prophetic books give, and it is the same concept that appears in Revelation.

The Distinction between Divine and Human Perspectives

Why does the Bible use terms like "soon" and "near" to refer to events that are actually far in the future? A part of the solution lies in the fact that a difference exists between the divine and human perspectives. God wishes to reveal *what* He intends to do without revealing *when* and *how* He will do it (1 Pet. 1:10–12).[55] The *what*-ness of prophecy provides all the application that the church

---

the 'last days' and even the 'last hour' have been ongoing for almost two thousand years" ("A Critique of the Preterist View of 'Soon' and 'Near,'" 476).

[55] "Circumstances of time and manner may remain indefinite in prophecy without prejudice to the reality of the events predicted." John T. Curran, "The Teaching of II Peter 1:20 on the Interpretation of Prophecy," *Theological Studies* 4, no. 3 (September 1943): 361.

needs, regardless of when those events will occur. In this regard the idealist's desire to find immediate applicability for the church is noble, even if his method is mistaken. The facts of God's divine communication are the substance of doctrine, reproof, correction, and instruction in righteousness whether or not the individual believer sees the events of prophecy unfold with his own eyes. Proof of this statement is so abundant that it is staggering to hear so many interpreters insist otherwise. Men and women of faith often did not receive the promises (Heb. 11:13) but still profited from the prophecies that they had received. The Old Testament is full of unrealized hopes, unmet expectations, and unfulfilled promises. Therefore, the assertion that unless the prophecy finds a complete fulfillment in its immediate audience, it has no value or application for that audience contradicts Scripture. From God's perspective these events are not only certain and true but also sequential. From the human perspective these events are certain and true. Sometimes we know their sequence. Sometimes we do not.

Observing the distinction between divine and human perspectives that is revealed in Old Testament prophecy, we can see how "near" and "soon" can indicate imminence rather than temporal immediacy (see figure 3). If Y and Z are distinct events in historical time that must happen (1) in order and (2) are therefore separated by some known or unknown interval of time, then Z cannot occur until Y has occurred. As long as Y has not occurred, Z remains sequentially "distant." As soon as Y occurs, Z becomes sequentially "near" whether or not it follows Y immediately. Any number of intervening historical years may exist between Y and Z, but this does not mitigate the fact that Z is now "near" in the sense of sequence. In the figure below, Y represents the death, burial, resurrection, and ascension of Christ, and Z represents His reign. The Old Testament prophets stood in position X (a period spanning over 1000 years from Moses to Malachi). To them, both Y and Z looked distant, and neither Y nor Z looked any more distant than the other. It is very important to remember that God did not reveal the sequential ordering of Y and Z to the prophets. *He* knew that Y must precede Z, but as far as the prophets were concerned *both* Y and Z were imminent. John wrote Revelation from a position after Y. From both the divine and human perspectives, Z was now "near" in sequential distance regardless of how far it was in historical distance.

FIGURE 3—THE CONCEPT OF DISTANCE IN PROPHETIC TIME

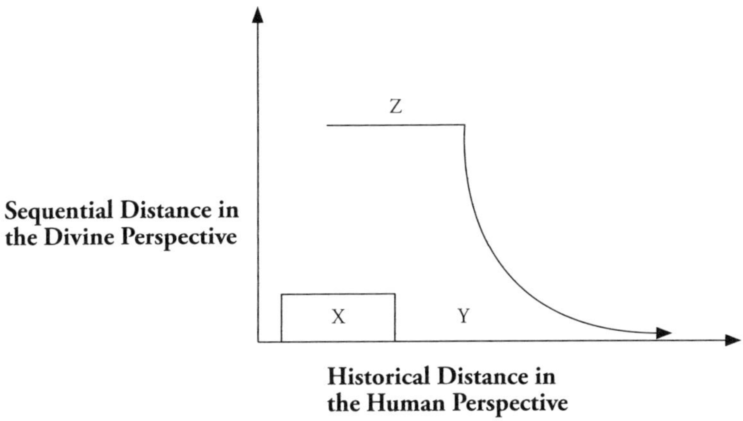

The next question to arise should be, can this scheme be justified from Scripture, or is it merely a convenient and creative solution to a prophetic problem? The following facts are crucial to the case.

1. The Old Testament prophets (human perspective) were apparently not directly aware of the separation of the cross and the crown of Christ in time (1 Pet. 1:10–12).[56] God did not

[56] Some of the prophets could have inferred that "the cross before the crown" was a necessary order that worked out repeatedly in the lives of typological figures including Abraham, Joseph, Moses, and David. Jesus implies that such an inference would have been appropriate (Luke 24:25–26). However, the Old Testament lacks explicit statements that divide Christ's two comings.

communicate to them a distinction in the comings of Christ. The prophetic accounts are often seamless in blending both comings of Christ.

2. The prophets (human perspective) view the events associated with Christ's kingship as imminent. All of the events (Y and Z) seem to have the same horizon.

3. The New Testament indicates (post-ascension) that we are already living in the last days (divine perspective) and, therefore, that the events associated with Christ's final kingship (Z) are now imminent.

4. The fact that the prophets treated events (Z), which we now know to have been sequential, as "near" indicates conclusively that "nearness" of time in prophecy pertains to imminence and not merely proximity.

No conservative seriously questions points 1 and 3 above. Points 2 and 4 create a sticking point, however. Can we demonstrate that the prophets viewed events that are *still* unfulfilled as imminent, and does such a demonstration use the same terminology that appears in Revelation? If so, then Revelation's references to "soon" and "near" would likely indicate imminence rather than immediacy.

The most frequent expression in which the term *near* appears (ἐγγύς in the Septuagint; קרום, *qrwm* in Hebrew) occurs in the phrase "the day of the Lord is near" (see table 8 below). Although we do not know the time frame in every instance, most of the "day of the Lord" prophecies have a time gap between prophecy and fulfillment of over 2,600 years. In prophetic contexts, then, "near"-ness of time does not mean immediacy. It has to mean imminence.

Table 8—"Near" in Prophetic Contexts

Passage	Referent
Isaiah 13:6 Howl ye; for the day of the Lord *is* at hand; it shall come as a destruction from the Almighty.	Ultimate destruction of Babylon, 2700+ years time gap
Ezekiel 30:3 For the day *is* near, even the day of the Lord *is* near, a cloudy day; it shall be the time of the heathen.	Destruction of Egypt by Babylon, unknown time gap
Joel 1:15 Alas for the day! for the day of the Lord *is* at hand, and as a destruction from the Almighty shall it come.	Locust plague or future judgment, unknown time gap
Joel 2:1 Blow ye the trumpet in Zion, and sound an alarm in my holy mountain: let all the inhabitants of the land tremble: for the day of the Lord cometh, for *it is* nigh at hand.	Uncertain military invasion, either Babylon or distant future, time gap of 11–2600+ years
Joel 3:14 Multitudes, multitudes in the valley of decision: for the day of the Lord *is* near in the valley of decision.	Armageddon, time gap of 2600+ years
Obadiah 1:15 For the day of the Lord *is* near upon all the heathen: as thou hast done, it shall be done unto thee: thy reward shall return upon thine own head.	Destruction of all nations, time gap of 2800+ years?
Zephaniah 1:7 Hold thy peace at the presence of the Lord God: for the day of the Lord *is* at hand: for the Lord hath prepared a sacrifice, he hath bid his guests.	Destruction of all the earth, time gap of 2600+ years
Zephaniah 1:14 The great day of the Lord *is* near, *it is* near, and hasteth greatly, *even* the voice of the day of the Lord: the mighty man shall cry there bitterly.	

Some interpreters believe that Old Testament prophecy relies heavily upon the use of hyperbole (conscious exaggeration that the writer does not intend his reader to take literally) in its description of both judgment and blessing. Obviously, if we interpret literally what the writer intends hyperbolically, we will misinterpret the text. However, as a literary device, hyperbole must be unmistakably clear in order to be effective.

We would never mistake the statement, "I'm older than the hills and twice as tough," for a literal claim. But to spiritualize prophecy as a whole by claiming that the prophets abound in this literary device oversteps the evidence. When God says, "And the house of Jacob shall be a fire, and the house of Joseph a flame, and the house of Esau for stubble, and they shall kindle in them, and devour them; and there shall not be any remaining of the house of Esau; for the Lord hath spoken it" (Obad. 18), the context neither requires nor encourages a hyperbolic interpretation.

The evidence from Old Testament prophecy is that the futurist has not overstated his case or made up a convenient or extreme interpretation of "soon" and "near" in Revelation. These terms have a long-standing meaning of imminence when connected with prophecy, the future, and divine judgment.

Summary

The implications should be obvious. Nothing in this argument proves that Preterism, Historicism, and Idealism are wrong. This argument does demonstrate, however, that one of the single strongest attacks that these systems can launch against Futurism is flawed. It is biblically refutable, and such a refutation requires no manipulation of data or creative exegesis. It requires only that the exegete recognize that when God brings an event "near" to mankind, that nearness does not require immediate fulfillment. It means that the fulfillment is imminent.

Relevance for Its Recipients

A second charge that critics make against Futurism concerns its apparent lack of value for a first-century audience. If the fulfillment of these events lies two thousand years or more into the future, what value does that have for suffering Christians in the past? Gentry gives a voice to this position when he states, "It almost totally removes the relevance of Revelation from John's original audience, especially at a time of their great suffering."[57] Idealism and even Historicism concur with this assessment. Lenski, an

[57] "A Preterist View," 92.

idealist, claims that if we accept the futurist position, "Revelation has little direct value for the church prior to the last few years of its existence."[58] All three of these systems urge a perspective that seeks relevance for the first-century recipient.

Futurism responds with a two-pronged answer. First, in the attempt to meet the "felt needs" of God's people, preachers and teachers often mishandle Scripture. It is better to accept the Lord's assessment of relevance rather than to impose a relevance that is foreign to the text. That God chose to reveal the distant future to a persecuted church should cause us to reconsider our humanistic notions of relevance. He understands what persecuted people need to hear. Second, the charge of Revelation's irrelevance-if-prophetic should astonish any conservative interpreter. Were the prophecies concerning the Messiah irrelevant to the age in which they were given? When Isaiah prophesied about the coming of Christ, this event was seven hundred years distant. Are we to concur with charges that determine the relevance of a biblical prophecy on the basis of its fulfillment in one's own generation? Then maybe Genesis 3:15 was irrelevant to Adam and Eve, since the birth of Messiah would not come for at least four thousand years. Prophecy derives its relevance from the fact that God speaks to His people when, how, and for what reason He intends. All other relevance fades into insignificance. The charge that Futurism lacked relevance for the first-century, persecuted church stands contrary to Scripture and reason.

Verifiability and Falsifiability

Some commentators complain that Futurism places itself beyond the pale of testability and cannot therefore be considered

---

[58] R. C. H. Lenski, *The Interpretation of St. John's Revelation*, Commentary on the New Testament (Augsburg, 1963; repr., Peabody, MA: Hendrickson Publishers, 1998), 215.

philosophically or theologically viable.[59] Modern scientific and philosophical arguments tend to define the supernatural out of existence preemptively. By setting the terms of the debate, science precludes any solution except materialistic naturalism. Philosophy attempts the same when it interacts with biblical prophecy and requires falsifiability as a test for viability. Since the ultimate Author of Revelation has already fulfilled hundreds of other prophecies that He made in the distant past, His track record of historical verification is well established—as long as the book applies literally.[60] If the book were entirely or predominantly symbolic, then Futurism might lack adequate philosophical warrant for its assertions.

Conclusion

Among the major interpretive systems that seek to explain the book of Revelation, Futurism stands out as the system that coheres with Old Testament prophecy and a normal hermeneutic, that operates with the greatest internal coherence and consistency, and that rebuts the charges of its detractors most decisively. These observations strongly favor Futurism without requiring hyperliteralism and without dismissing the symbolism that occurs in Revelation.

---

[59] Gentry gives voice to this charge: "It is not subject to historical verification presently and thus is incapable of falsification; in this way it fails the philosophical verification principle, which according to some philosophers renders it philosophically meaningless" ("A Preterist View," 92).

[60] After writing this section I found this idea of past verification corroborated in Paul Lee Tan, *The Interpretation of Prophecy* (Ann Arbor: Cushing-Malloy, 1974), 62.

3

The Millennium

One of the most significant questions that believers ask concerning the future is whether or not Christ will set up His kingdom on this earth in fulfillment of His promises to Israel. Conservative Christians concur that when God creates a new heaven and a new earth, He will dwell with His people forever, but they do not agree on whether Christ will have a literal, earthly reign prior to the eternal state. This chapter explores the millennial positions and defends Premillennialism as the most natural interpretation of Revelation 20.

Definition and Distinctions of the Millennial Systems

The definitions cited for each of the millennial systems derive from the proponents of the systems or from citations with which its proponents agree. This prevents a mis-defining of a term by its opponents.

Amillennialism

Postmillennial and premillennial writers treat Amillennialism as an anti-system. They observe that it has no self-defined systematic presentation of the future. Part of this critique stems from the fact that since Amillennialism asserts a strongly spiritual method and exhibits a strongly anti-material bias, it cannot produce a Millennium that matches the Bible's literal description of that kingdom. The system's interpretive presuppositions disallow an organized portrayal of the future in anything other than the broadest terms. Louis Berkhof, an amillennialist, concurs:

> The Amillennial view is, as the name indicates, purely negative. It holds that there is no sufficient Scriptural ground for the expectation of a millennium, and is firmly convinced that the Bible favors the idea that the present dispensation of the Kingdom of God will be followed *immediately* by the Kingdom of God in its consummate and eternal form.[1]

Berkhof illustrates the anti-systematic quality of Amillennialism by devoting the rest of his chapter to an attack on Premillennialism. He gives no space to developing the Amillennialism to which he holds. Since Amillennialism denies that the Scripture places any events (Tribulation, resurrections, Millennium) between the present age and the age to come, it obviously cannot address these beliefs in a positive fashion. William Cox cites Walvoord's definition approvingly:

> A good definition of amillennialism comes from the pen of one of its severest critics. "Its most general character is that of denial of a literal reign of Christ upon earth. Satan is conceived as bound at the first coming of Christ. The present age between the first and second comings is the fulfillment of the millennium. Its adherents are divided on whether the millennium is being fulfilled now on earth (Augustine) or whether it is being fulfilled by the saints in heaven (Kliefoth). It may be summed up in the idea that there will be no more millennium than there is now, and

[1] Louis Berkhof, *Systematic Theology*, combined ed. (Grand Rapids: Eerdmans, 1996), 708.

> that the eternal state immediately follows the second coming of Christ."[2]

In one sense it is not fair to require Amillennialism to develop a system in a realm of theology that it believes does not exist. This would be like asking a seventeenth-century scientist to develop in detail a system explaining germ theory. The germ non-believer cannot explain the details of germs. His only recourse is to an anti-system.

The question remains: Is the amillennial denial of the reality of the literal, earthly Millennium adequately warranted? Let's return to our analogy and ask, is the germ non-believer's denial of the reality of germs adequately warranted? Assuming we had a detailed germ theory manual from the future, the answer would be no. But it is also understandable why the germ non-believer would reject the manual from the future. He could assume that it was a fraud. He could assume that it was an imaginative speculation or vague symbol to describe the unknown. His assumption could be wrong even while it retained a sense of viability and respectability. A person does not become a science-hater just because he thinks the evidence is too shallow to warrant a change in his belief. On the other hand his personal disbelief does not overthrow the accuracy of modern germ theory.

Postmillennialism and Premillennialism both disagree with the amillennial claim that "there is no sufficient Scriptural ground for the expectation of a millennium." In addition, Premillennialism insists on "a literal reign of Christ upon earth" and denies that "Satan is conceived as bound at the first coming of Christ" or that

[2] See John. F. Walvoord, *The Millennial Kingdom* (Findley, OH: Dunham Publishing Company, 1959), 6. William E. Cox picks up on Walvoord's definition and assumes it as accurately describing Amillennialism in *Amillennialism Today*, 1.

"the present age between the first and second comings is the fulfillment of the millennium."

Postmillennialism

"Postmillennialism is that view of the last things which holds that the kingdom of God is now being extended in the world through the preaching of the gospel and the saving work of the Holy Spirit in the hearts of individuals, that the world eventually is to be Christianized and that the return of Christ is to occur at the close of a long period of righteousness and peace commonly called the millennium."[3]

Amillennialism and Premillennialism agree with the first half of this definition, but they take issue with the claim that "the world eventually is to be Christianized." Premillennialists also balk at the claim that "the return of Christ is to occur at the close of . . . the millennium."

Premillennialism

In its simplest form, "Premillennialism teaches that the second coming of Jesus Christ to the earth takes place before (pre) the millennial reign."[4] Premillennialism relies on a normal, literal interpretation of prophecy. It also argues that Scripture indicates an increase in wickedness and apostasy as the age draws to a close. Typically the system also teaches that the purposes of the Millennium include fulfilling Old Testament promises to Israel

---

[3] Loraine Boettner, "Postmillennialism," in *The Meaning of the Millennium*, 117. In addition, Boettner contends, "The postmillennialist looks for a golden age that will not be essentially different from our own so far as the basic facts of life are concerned. This age gradually merges into the millennial age as an increasing proportion of the world's inhabitants are converted to Christianity" (Ibid., 120).

[4] Paul N. Benware, *Understanding End Times Prophecy: A Comprehensive Approach* (Chicago: Moody Press, 1995), 92.

and demonstrating the superiority of Christ's redemption to a perfect environment as the only adequate means of man's hope for salvation.

Amillennialism and Postmillennialism reject the premillennialist's understanding of the timing of Christ's return and the events surrounding that return. Both also reject the literal interpretation of prophecy to some extent, although some postmillennialists are more consistent interpreters than amillennialists. Amillennialism utterly rejects the necessity of fulfilling Old Testament prophecies literally (and most postmillennialists concur). Both reject the premillennial understanding of the purposes for the Millennium.

COMPARATIVE INTERPRETATIONS OF REVELATION 20

Revelation 20 provides the clearest demonstration of the differences among these three systems. All three must account for the meaning of the first eight verses of this chapter. Table 9 below sketches what each system believes about this crucial passage. Some interpreters within a given system may tweak the data and present an interpretation slightly different from the one given below. However, this table summarizes the writings of the major interpreters for each system.

An examination of the table makes several crucial issues evident. Amillennialism and Postmillennialism agree almost perfectly in their interpretation of Revelation 20. Loraine Boettner, one of the foremost proponents of Postmillennialism in the twentieth century, concurs: "There is comparatively little difference between postmillennialism and amillennialism."[5] Proponents of both of these systems assert that Revelation 20 is the least clear of the passages

[5] Loraine Boettner, "A Postmillennial Response," in *The Meaning of the Millennium*, 199.

of Scripture concerning the future, but they cannot establish this statement by anything other than an appeal to the symbolic quality of apocalyptic literature. The premillennialist begins to suspect that such an appeal derives less from the actual opaqueness of the passage and more from the fact that the passage is so clear that it disestablishes both Amillennialism and Postmillennialism. As noted previously, interpretive method affects the outcome exceedingly. Normal interpretation necessitates a premillennial outcome. The next section addresses the interpretations cited in this chart.

Table 9—Revelation 20 & a Comparison of Systems

	Amillennialism	Postmillennialism	Premillennialism
Assessment of Passage	The meaning is unclear	The meaning is unclear	The meaning is clear
Placement of the Passage in the Structure of Revelation	Beginning another recapitulatory cycle; merely repeats the same information as the earlier sections of Rev.	Beginning another recapitulatory cycle; merely repeats the same information as the earlier sections of Rev.	Follows the essentially linear progress of the book in placing the Millennium after the Second Coming
Placement of the Passage in Time	Entire church age	Entire church age	Following the Tribulation
Interpretation Method	Spiritual-symbolic	Spiritual-symbolic	Literal
Transmission	A vision, not reality	A vision, not reality	A vision, but real
Binding of Satan (shut him up; set a seal)	Figurative—he cannot prevent the spread of the gospel	Figurative—a slowly increasing restriction of his evil plan	A literal binding with a type of chain fitting for a spiritual being; a genuine removal from all ability to influence the people of the earth
One Thousand	Symbolic of completeness	Symbolic of completeness	Literal 1,000 years
The Abyss	Usually ignored; when interpreted it is figurative—not a real location, redundant with his being restricted	Ignored	An actual location that appears not only here but in Rev. 9:1–2; 11:7; 17:8

	Amillennialism	Postmillennialism	Premillennialism
Souls of the Beheaded	Disembodied spirits in heaven	Disembodied spirits in heaven	Dead believers who are about to be re-clothed with life for an earthly reign
They Lived	Spiritual life/salvation	Spiritual life/salvation	Physical life
First Resurrection	Totally different in type and consequence from the second resurrection	Totally different in type and consequence from the second resurrection	The same in type (bodily) as the second resurrection; different in consequence

A Case for Premillennialism

A work of this brevity cannot provide a complete defense of the arguments for the premillennial position.[6] Rather, this section treats a few of the most significant arguments that favor a premillennial interpretation. Premillennialism seems to be a lightning rod in the debate. Post- and amillennialists spend comparatively few pages defending their own systems or attacking each other.[7] Instead they invest the bulk of their energies assaulting Premillennialism. Although these attacks seem out of proportion, they make sense. Neither post- nor amillennial interpretations threaten each other very much. Since they agree on a "symbolic" method of interpretation, the subjective impression of the reader guides him toward one or the other interpretation. Each of the two systems feels that it offers a better explanation of the spiritualized events, but each lacks the explanatory power that would draw large numbers of

[6] Much literature exists to argue this case more thoroughly, providing further information for the inquisitive reader. See, for example, Charles L. Feinberg, *Millennialism: The Two Major Views* (Chicago: Moody Bible Institute, 1936; repr., BMH Books, 2008); Donald K. Campbell and Jeffrey L. Townsend, eds. *A Case for Premillennialism: A New Consensus* (Chicago: Moody Press, 1992); J. Dwight Pentecost, *Things to Come: A Study in Biblical Eschatology* (Grand Rapids: Zondervan Publishing House, 1958); and John F. Walvoord, *The Millennial Kingdom.*

[7] Loraine Boettner's lengthy treatment, *The Millennium* (Grand Rapids: Baker Book House, 1958), illustrates this perfectly. In a 375-page book Boettner defends his own Postmillennialism in 105 pages (28%); he addresses Amillennialism in 31 pages (8%); then he spends 239 pages attacking Premillennialism (64%).

people toward its respective system. On the other hand the insistently normal interpretation of Premillennialism, if correct, spells the death of the other two systems. Once the reader accepts the predominantly literal method, he cannot arrive at either Post- or Amillennialism. Thus, Premillennialism ranks as the primary target.

Summary Arguments

Some of the arguments for Premillennialism overlap those made for the futurist position in the preceding chapter. For example, the church held a chiliast interpretation of Revelation during its first two centuries of existence. Only after philosophy made inroads into the church did it abandon both the literal method and a premillennial interpretation of Revelation. Attempts to dismiss Premillennialism as a novelty or a recent phenomenon fly in the face of church history.

Premillennialism also holds to the consistency of the Old Testament covenants and prophecy as presented in appendix 1, which supports the argument for literal interpretation. The same applies here. If the covenants and prophecies of Scripture have a literal fulfillment at all, Premillennialism must be the correct interpretation of Revelation. This claim may sound like grandstanding, but even the critics of Premillennialism admit as much.

The Admissions of Critics

Given a literal method of interpretation, Premillennialism *must* be true. That statement sounds like one that only a premillennialist could make, but it actually finds corroboration in the opponents of Premillennialism. Robert L. Thomas observes, "Kuyper acknowledges that the language of Revelation 20:1–10 found anywhere else [in the Bible] would require literal interpretation, but he thinks that its surroundings in this book require the terminology to be understood nonliterally."[8]

Anthony Hoekema admits that if one assumes a literal interpretation, "We are then virtually compelled to believe that the thousand-year reign depicted in 20:4 must come after the return of Christ described in 19:11."[9]

Floyd Hamilton agrees: "Now we must frankly admit that a literal interpretation of the Old Testament prophecies gives us just such a picture of an earthly reign of the Messiah as the premillennialist pictures. That was the kind of a Messianic kingdom that the Jews of the time of Christ were looking for, on the basis of a literal interpretation of the Old Testament."[10] This comment indicates that the Jews' interpretation of the Old Testament was a natural interpretation. That God so configured His Word to mislead His people in their expectations of the entire nature of His promised kingdom is inconceivable to the premillennialist. The biblical situation is not simply a matter of naïve or obstinate Jews' misunderstanding clear truth due to their jaded beliefs. The disciples were among those who interpreted the Old Testament prophecies in exactly this fashion, and Jesus never rebutted their beliefs.

As a liberal, R. H. Charles rejects the authority of Scripture, but he admits, "In point of fact there are interpreters who, while applying the Eschatological Method rightly on the whole, treat everything relating to Chiliasm in our author purely symbolically. But the prophecy of the Millennium in chap. xx must be taken

[8] Thomas, "Literary Genre and Hermeneutics of the Apocalypse," 104.

[9] Anthony A. Hoekema, "Amillennialism," in *The Meaning of the Millennium: Four Views*, 156. He observes that literal interpretation leads to (1) a futurist and (2) a chronological view of Revelation.

[10] Floyd Hamilton, *The Basis of Millennial Faith* (Grand Rapids: Eerdmans, 1942), 38.

literally, as it was by Justin Martyr, Irenaeus, Victorinus of Pettau. These writers were acquainted with the original interpretation of this chapter."[11] Normal interpretation produces the premillennial position.

The Interpretation of Revelation 20

The premillennial interpretation of this important chapter surpasses the coherence and naturalness of the other two systems. It follows the text closely and argues that nothing in the text or near context warrants spiritualizing the passage. Taken naturally, the text coheres with biblical doctrine. It introduces no contradictions and violates no rules of grammar or logic. It meets the qualifications of Ockham's razor since it proposes no new methods or solutions that are not already inherent in the text.[12] The other systems require (1) a spiritual method, (2) an unnatural time referent to the church age, (3) a non-textual definition of what the binding of Satan entails, (4) a spiritualizing of the duration of the Millennium, (5) an ignoring of the abyss, (6) an unnatural splitting of the meaning of *resurrection*, and (7) a dissociation of the thought flow from Revelation 19 to 20.

Within the context of Revelation 20, Premillennialism does not need to appeal to complex explanations. An angel descends from heaven, binds Satan, throws him into the abyss (a location that is decidedly not earth), and seals him in for one thousand actual years. Dead saints rise (notice that their resurrection looks back to

---

[11] R. H. Charles, *Revelation of St John*, 1:clxxxiv.

[12] *Ockham's razor* is the assessment that when two or more competing theories seem to be able to explain the data, the theory that resorts to the fewest new assumptions is superior to the others. That is, when a theory introduces unnatural elements into the equation in order for the system to "work" in its natural setting, the unprejudiced observer will reject it in favor of a theory that does not resort to "convenient" explanations unnatural to the setting.

their being killed by the beast bodily) and reign with Christ for this same one thousand years, and the rest of the dead stay dead until after this one thousand years is past. Then Satan returns from his captivity and stirs up rebellion again.

Attempts to rebut this position fail. For example, a chain does not have to be made from steel in order to be literal. A chain is an instrument of binding that is appropriate to the context of the person or object needing to be chained.

Postmillennialism and Amillennialism draw on Matthew 12:25–30 as proof that Satan's binding is a figurative binding that prevents him from blocking the spread of the gospel. However, Satan's binding in Revelation 20 does not match the illustration that Jesus gives in Matthew 12:25–30.[13] Jesus addresses (1) demon possession (2) of an individual (3) where the location of the demon's binding is unrecorded (4) the result of which is freedom from demon possession (5) for the present life. Revelation 20 addresses (1) Satan's freedom (2) to deceive all the nations (3) where Satan's binding occurs in the abyss (4) the result of which is reign of truth in the millennial kingdom (5) for one thousand years. Notice what the spiritual interpreter must do. He has to spiritualize the freedom of individuals from demon possession (the clear referent of the passage in Matthew), make this spiritualized interpretation the point of Matthew's text, and then spiritualize Revelation 20 to match his other spiritualization. None of these interpretive actions find warrant in the passages at hand.

---

[13] This verse in Matthew is the primary interpretive warrant for spiritualizing Revelation 20's binding of Satan, but the situations are far too dissimilar to warrant the tenuous connection that Post- and Amillennialism make.

Revelation presents three essential locations: heaven, earth, and otherworldly places of judgment (including the abyss, hell, and the lake of fire). That an angel binds Satan in the abyss manifestly indicates his removal from the earth. The interpreter cannot erode such a clear spatial distinction without jeopardizing all interpretive controls.

The first and second resurrections are not different by virtue of a spiritual versus physical quality. Two textual evidences indicate this fact. First, the same terminology applies to both resurrections, leading the reader to seek some other basis for their difference. Since the second resurrection is clearly a bodily resurrection unto judgment, the first resurrection is also best interpreted as a bodily resurrection unto the reigning with Christ. Second, the text juxtaposes the death of these "souls" with their coming to life within the same verse (v. 4)! Their death was an indisputably bodily death, and their coming to life most naturally matches their martyrdom.

The most natural explanation of Revelation 20 is also the simplest, and yet its simplicity does not reduce its doctrinal accuracy or its ability to explain eschatology. The other interpretive systems have yet to produce an adequate warrant for their handling of this crucial passage.[14]

[14] Gentry goes so far as to say, "I would prefer to leave Revelation 20 out of my presentation. It plays too prominent a role in the eschatological debate, overshadowing much clearer passages and bringing confusion into the debate" Kenneth L. Gentry Jr., "Postmillennialism," in *Three Views on the Millennium and Beyond*, ed. Darrell L. Bock, Counterpoints, ed. Stanley N. Gundry (Grand Rapids: Zondervan, 1999), 51. Clarity is not the issue. Revelation 20 provides as clear an indication as possible concerning the timing, duration, and select qualities of the Millennium. Rather, the post- and amillennialists cannot warrant their conclusions in Revelation 20. Having rejected the completely obvious, transparent meaning of the chapter, these systems would rather leave Rev. 20 out of the discussion entirely if possible.

Answers to Charges against Premillennialism

We can measure the workability of a system in part by how well it can answer the charges of its critics. Premillennialism passes this test by demonstrating that it is solidly biblical.

Premillennialism Is Unspiritual and Materialistic

The charge of materialism hardly warrants an answer. It derives from dualistic philosophy that has threatened the church since its early days. Gnostics regularly taught that matter was evil and spirit was good. God had no interaction with the material world, since He was far too pure to dabble with ordinary matter. Because of its seeming spirituality, this type of thinking has plagued the church repeatedly. While it holds to part of the truth (this present world system is evil and allied against God), its imprecision leads to abuses (anything material is evil). The best answer requires the interpreter to start at the very beginning: "In the beginning God created the heavens and the earth." The material world did not arise in rebellion. Satan did not create it. Insubordinate man did not form it. God created matter and the earth. Moreover, He promises to restore the physical order in a new heavens and new earth. This hope appears in both the Old and New Testaments (Isa. 65:17; 66:22; 2 Pet. 3:13; Rev. 21:1). The fact that these references apply to the eternal state strengthens the case—matter is not evil. Premillennialism simply recognizes that for His own purposes God has chosen to demonstrate His power, glory, justice, and salvation through the immediate reign of Christ on this earth for a period prior to the eternal state. Human philosophy may question that possibility, but Scripture does not.

Premillennialism Replaces the Church with Israel

If true, the charge that Premillennialism replaces the church with Israel certainly would threaten the clear doctrine of the New Testament.[15] Premillennialism in no way diminishes the church any more than Christ's relationship to the Father diminishes Christ's person. The recognition that God has different roles, different covenants, in different times, and in different ways for different institutions (Israel/church) does not diminish one in favor of the other.

In fact, the New Testament seems to indicate that the greater threat lies in the church's arrogance against Israel and in its attempt to appropriate God's promises to Israel. Romans 11:18–29 addresses this theme repeatedly:

> Boast not against the branches. . . . Thou wilt say then, The branches were broken off, that I might be graffed in. . . . I would not, brethren, that ye should be ignorant of this mystery, lest ye should be wise in your own conceits; that blindness in part is happened to Israel, until the fulness of the Gentiles be come in. And so all Israel shall be saved: as it is written, There shall come out of Sion the Deliverer, and shall turn away ungodliness from Jacob: for this is my covenant unto them, when I shall take away their sins. As concerning the gospel, they are enemies for your sakes: but as touching the election, they are beloved for the fathers' sakes. For the gifts and calling of God are without repentance.

[15] Ironically, many who raise this charge don't seem concerned about Israel's replacement by the church. Somehow that seems less anti-doctrinal than the reverse.

"Boast" and "conceits" apply directly to the church when it acts ignorantly of its own mystery status and tries to deny God's promises to Israel. The passage could not be clearer. Much sophistry has appeared in the course of church history to do away with this passage. Sadly, that sophistry has violated the very warning of the passage. God has a place for Israel in the future not because she deserves it, but because He has promised it. He will turn Israel nationally from her sins in accordance with Jeremiah 31:31–34. Premillennialists do not claim to understand all of God's purposes with reference to the church. They know that Israel will not replace the church, but they also know that the church has not replaced Israel in national terms.

When Premillennialism handles the new man of Ephesians 2:14–16, it notes that the passage does not indicate a transformation of Israel into the church or the church into Israel. It does not say that the church is spiritual Israel. It says that Christ has formed a new man that consists of Jews and Gentiles. Formerly, the most important consideration of a Jew was his Jewishness. Now it is his identity in Christ. Ephesians 2 does not get rid of Israel or Gentiles. It also does not comment on eschatology and what God intends to do with Israel, the Gentiles, and the church in the future. It simply describes the present spiritual newness that all believers possess in Christ. The assumption that Israel equals the church or that the church has permanently replaced Israel and therefore God cannot have any special plan for Israel in the future goes far beyond appropriate exegesis of this passage.

Premillennialism Fails to See the Spiritualization of Old Testament Prophecy

This point serves as the basis for the preceding. If the church inherits the covenants made between God and Israel, then presumably resuming those covenants with Israel would be stealing them from the church. However, there is little warrant for the claim that the church inherits the covenants made with Israel. The church experiences blessings in line with the covenants insofar as several Old Testament covenants extended grace to the Gentiles. Moreover, since Romans 11 denies that God's covenants with Israel are revocable, God's fulfillment of kingdom promises to Israel in the future should remain our expectation.

A corresponding charge is that the literalism evident within premillennial thought is the same kind of literalism that led the Pharisees to crucify Jesus.[16] The charge is absurd. First, the Pharisees' own mouths condemned them. They crucified Jesus because His kingdom threatened their personal power over the people. They literally interpreted the fact that the Messiah was to be born in Bethlehem of Judea (and they were correct), but they did not care. Hyperliteralism was not the problem. Their hearts had become spiritually dull (Matt. 13:14–15). To turn the tables on the spiritualizer, they crucified Jesus because they *rejected* the literal interpretation of Old Testament prophecy concerning the Messiah's meekness, unobtrusiveness, humility, and sacrifice. Their problem was not the hyperliteralizing of Old Testament prophecy; it was their refusal to accept God's plan at all.

For each supposed failure of Premillennialism to see the New Testament spiritualization of prophecy, a better, more contextually sound exegesis exists. For example, Boettner claims that

[16] I am not exaggerating this claim. Cox calls the premillennial position "hyperliteralism" and then says, "Hyperliteralism is the same interpretation given to certain passages from the Old Testament by the Pharisees of Jesus' day. It was this method of interpretation that, humanly speaking, kept them from recognizing the Christ as the Hope of Israel. Hyperliteralism kept them from seeing that the unfulfilled promises of the Old Testament were to be fulfilled through the Christian church" (23).

Galatians 3:7 spiritualizes the Old Testament and makes the church equal Israel.[17] But is this really what Galatians 3:7 says? Not at all. The Old Testament indicates that Abraham would have a physical seed through which all nations (spiritual seed) would be blessed. Galatians 3:7 does not (1) reject Israel as the (source of the) physical seed, (2) make the church Israel, or (3) spiritualize the Old Testament promise to Abraham as something new. How do we know? Because verse 8 tells us so! The only provision of the Abrahamic Covenant that the church fulfills is the promise that Abraham would have a spiritual seed, but then again, we already knew that from Genesis. Not a shred of "spiritualization" of Old Testament prophecy has occurred here. Boettner has simply interpreted in a manner calculated to bolster a symbolic method that otherwise lacks adequate warrant.

Some writers argue that the intersection of Galatians 3:28–29 and Ephesians 2:14–16 warrants the application of Old Testament prophecy to the church. Surely these passages make the church Israel. Not at all. These passages address the creation of a "new man." There is a "third something" here that the Old Testament did not explain. The Old Testament told us *that* there would be a spiritual seed of Abraham, but it did not lay out exactly *how* that spiritual seed would be integrated. The Jews assumed that Gentiles participated in this facet of the Abrahamic Covenant by becoming proselytes. No one suspected that God had a "new man" organism planned. In Christ, a new body exists. Jews and Gentiles participate in this "new man," which is the church. But the church is not Israel or even spiritual Israel. Those who are spiritual Israel are in the church. It is fallacious to assume that if one party is a subset of the other, the two are identical. Galatians 3:27 indicates that

[17] Boettner, "A Postmillennial Response," 51.

Jews and Gentiles share in the new oneness in Christ. Ephesians 2:14–16 indicates that Jew and Gentile are united in one "new man . . . in one body."

Premillennialism deals very carefully with prophecy. It guards the natural, original referents against a tendency toward unwarranted reinterpretation. It recognizes that Christ and the apostles held a uniquely authoritative status in their use and application of the Old Testament to the situation that surrounded them, but it insists that we do not have the authority to take a dubious and ill-established interpretive principle and apply it broadly to the Old Testament.

Premillennialism Has Only Six Verses of Support

That Revelation 20 is the only passage to specify the length of the Millennium has absolutely no biblical or logical weight against its literal accuracy. Yet critics regularly and insistently trumpet this as proof that Premillennialism is hyperliteral and stubbornly wrong.[18] The assumption, of course, is that numbers in Scripture have symbolic significance, especially in books of prophecy. Besides the fact that this assumption itself remains unproven,[19] the Bible actually throws its weight behind the premillennial interpretation. In the Old Testament, the prophecy concerning the length of Judah's captivity in Babylon appears in only two chapters (and only

[18] "The only place in the entire Bible where the millennium is mentioned per se is in Revelation" (Cox, 63). "This passage is the only place in the Bible which speaks of a millennium" (Anthony A. Hoekema, "An Amillennial Response," in *The Meaning of the Millennium: Four Views*, 55). "The only place in all of Scripture associating a period of one thousand years with the reign of Christ is this first half of this single chapter. If a literal earthly Millennium is such an important and glorious era in redemptive history (as premillennialists argue), then it is odd that reference to the thousand years should appear in only one passage in all of Scripture" (Kenneth L. Gentry Jr., "Postmillennialism," 51).

[19] See the argument to the contrary in John J. Davis, *Biblical Numerology: A Basic Study of the Use of Numbers in the Bible* (Grand Rapids: Baker Book House, 1968).

three verses within those chapters: Jeremiah 25:11–12 and 29:10; incidentally, Revelation cites the Millennium in six verses or twice the support as Jeremiah's prophecy!).[20] Jeremiah's "seventy years" prophecy is also cited in one additional verse in regard to its fulfillment (Dan. 9:2). Since Daniel is one of those "apocalyptic books," we can summarily dismiss its testimony concerning the literality of events. Or can we? The question that the interpreter ought to grapple with is, how many times does God have to specify something in order for it to be true? When a passage does not contradict other Scripture and its literal meaning makes sense, the burden of proof for establishing an abnormal interpretation lies on the spiritual interpreter, not on the literal interpreter. In Jeremiah's prophecy God even specified a time period (70 years) that could easily be made symbolic (7 x 10) but was literal! Thus Jeremiah's prophecy presents an excellent test case in which a potentially numerically symbolic, seldom-mentioned prophecy of a specific future event found an exactly literal fulfillment. The Old Testament warrants the premillennial interpretation of Revelation.

The *duration* of the Millennium appears only in these six verses of Revelation, but the *expectation* of a kingdom that would look like Revelation's Messiah-centered earthly kingdom appears throughout the Scripture. In some passages this long-expected kingdom even relates directly to a time following severe tribulation for Israel and the world. Joel 3:9–21 provides a clear example:

> Proclaim ye this among the Gentiles; prepare war, wake up the mighty men, let all the men of war draw near; let them come up: beat your plowshares into swords, and your pruninghooks into spears: . . . The Lord also shall roar out

[20] See the additional evidence cited in the section "Observing the Fulfillment of Prophecy" in chapter 1.

> of Zion, and utter his voice from Jerusalem; and the heavens and the earth shall shake: but the Lord will be the hope of his people, and the strength of the children of Israel. So shall ye know that I am the Lord your God dwelling in Zion, my holy mountain: then shall Jerusalem be holy, and there shall no strangers pass through her any more. And it shall come to pass in that day, that the mountains shall drop down new wine, and the hills shall flow with milk, and all the rivers of Judah shall flow with waters, and a fountain shall come forth of the house of the Lord, and shall water the valley of Shittim. . . . Judah shall dwell for ever, and Jerusalem from generation to generation. For I will cleanse their blood that I have not cleansed: for the Lord dwelleth in Zion.

While we can appreciate the attempt of the amillennialist to make sense of this passage by connecting Joel 3 to the eternal state, passages such as Isaiah 65:17–25 indicate that death will still exist in this kingdom that is prior to the eternal state. Isaiah thus backs Revelation's temporal distinction between the millennial kingdom and the eternal kingdom (the new heavens and new earth).

> For, behold, I create new heavens and a new earth: and the former shall not be remembered, nor come into mind. But be ye glad and rejoice for ever in that which I create: for, behold, I create Jerusalem a rejoicing, and her people a joy. And I will rejoice in Jerusalem, and joy in my people: and the voice of weeping shall be no more heard in her, nor the voice of crying. There shall be no more thence an infant of days, nor an old man that hath not filled his days: for the child shall die an hundred years old; but the sinner being an hundred years old shall be accursed (Isa. 65:17–20).

We can also appreciate the care to observe that this passage in Isaiah mentions "new heavens and a new earth," which seems to reference the eternal state. Three options present themselves. Either we can recognize that God conflated many different time frames into individual prophetic images (sometimes called prophetic telescoping), or we can spiritualize the parts of the passage that do not fit our system, or we can ignore the parts of the passage that are inconvenient. Scripture actually corroborates the first of these methods. Just a few chapters earlier, Isaiah 61:1–4 says:

> The Spirit of the Lord God is upon me; because the Lord hath anointed me to preach good tidings unto the meek; he hath sent me to bind up the brokenhearted, to proclaim liberty to the captives, and the opening of the prison to them that are bound; to proclaim the acceptable year of the Lord, and the day of vengeance of our God; to comfort all that mourn; . . . And they shall build the old wastes, they shall raise up the former desolations, and they shall repair the waste cities, the desolations of many generations.

Jesus preached from this passage in His first recorded sermon at Nazareth in Luke 4:16–21. His treatment of the text indicates that although God revealed both comings of Christ to Isaiah in a single prophetic message, those comings of Christ would be separated by a long span of time that Isaiah apparently did not foresee.[21] In other words, the premillennial interpretation acknowledges how Daniel and Jesus handled prophecy and accepts an established method of interpretation over the spiritualization of difficult texts. Premillennialism makes the most sense of the whole corpus of

---

[21] 1 Pet. 1:11 indicates that the prophets did not understand the timing of Messiah's activities and may not have known how to fit Christ's suffering and glory together into a coherent picture.

prophecy without distorting the original context or its later application. The premillennial system has the support of far more than the first six verses of Revelation 20. It rests on the expectations of the prophets.

Premillennialism Interprets the Clear by the Opaque

The interpretation of the clear by the opaque, the simple by the more difficult, would be a reversal of the normal pattern of interpretation. If it were true, this argument would damage the premillennial position significantly. However, the "opaqueness" of Revelation depends on the extent to which the interpreter magnifies its symbolic quality. Of course the amillennialist finds Revelation 20 opaque. He made it so by his method of interpretation. Interpreted naturally, Revelation 20 is the clearest, though not the fullest, text on the Millennium. Amillennialism mistakes the shift from the incipient/partial expression of a truth to the final/complete expression of it for an issue of clear versus unclear. Thus, the amillennialist consistently argues that there can be only one general resurrection and only one general judgment at the end of the age, since the Old Testament and Gospels tell us that a resurrection and judgment are coming. Revelation 20 separates the resurrections and judgments. Again, we have several interpretive options: (1) we can accept the testimony of Revelation literally as part of the progressive quality of Scripture that does not contradict itself but further explains doctrine; (2) we can spiritualize the natural meaning of Revelation 20; or (3) we can reject the teaching of Revelation 20. Amillennialism and Postmillennialism choose the second option. Premillennialism believes that the clarity and order of Revelation 20 warrants and requires the first option.

Suppose that while telling a child how to play basketball, we said, "You shoot the ball into the basket. Whoever shoots the most baskets wins." Now suppose that someone else comes along later and says, "One team has to shoot down at that end of the court, and the other team has to shoot down at this end." If the child protests, "Your explanation is unclear. I have to interpret the unclear by the clear. My daddy told me that 'you shoot the ball into the basket.' He referred to only one basket, not two, and certainly not two that are separated by an intervening gap of space. I must reject your assertion that there are two baskets." The child's objection is neither accurate nor logically valid. The second account was neither contradictory nor more unclear. It was simply more developed.

Premillennialism interprets Revelation as it interprets all of Scripture. It sees Revelation as developing and expanding upon certain themes of Scripture through essentially literal communication. Revelation does not contradict the testimony of the Old or New Testaments when it takes the broad brush strokes of earlier writers and refines their focus or supplies additional details. It provides greater clarity, not greater obscurity.

Conclusion

The most natural interpretation of Revelation results in a premillennial position. Christians agree that Christ will come again as He said. Premillennialism observes that the timing and nature of this return as specified in Revelation 20 corroborate the Old Testament expectation of Christ's earthly rule on the throne of David. The age to come will break into the present age in a fashion not unlike Christ's first advent. In His first coming, the King was visibly at hand, and He exhibited the power of the age to come. His healing, casting out of demons, and turning the hearts of those who would believe toward God were indications that the future age had broken into the present. His substitutionary death opened redemption to mankind so that He might purchase a citizenry for His kingdom. In accordance with the expectations of a literal fulfillment of prophecy, Premillennialism awaits the return of the King Who will take possession of what is rightfully His.

4

The Revelation of Jesus Christ

Everything we have covered so far would cast a pale shadow of the proper interpretation of Revelation if we did not recognize Christ as the protagonist and His work as the theme and thesis of the book. Revelation does not present disinterested eschatology. It does not exist to titillate the imagination or to provoke either a self-centered pessimism or self-assured optimism. It does not make the church the center of God's purpose. Like the rest of Scripture, it points us to Christ. Several passages outside of Revelation warrant our search for Christ in every book of the Bible, and Revelation justifies this search.

> Search the scriptures; for in them ye think ye have eternal life: and they are they which testify of me (John 5:39).
>
> Then he said unto them, O fools, and slow of heart to believe all that the prophets have spoken: ought not Christ to have suffered these things, and to enter into his glory? And beginning at Moses and all the prophets, he expounded unto them in all the scriptures the things concerning himself (Luke 24:25–27).[1]

[1] This passage communicates an interesting point. The disciples' failure was not their hyperliteral acceptance of Old Testament prophecy but their refusal to accept *all* prophecy. They picked and chose what expectations they had concerning the Messiah. They decided in favor of an exclusively earthly King when the Old Testament told them that the Christ had to suffer. I believe that the spiritual/symbolic interpreter commits the same type of error. Denying the literal meaning of Old Testament prophecy is being "slow of heart to believe all that the prophets have spoken." Christ will yet do exactly

Since we are to believe "all that the prophets have spoken" concerning Christ, we ought to see in this final book of prophecy the person and work of our Prophet, Priest, and King.

Many liberal writers see the oppressed church as the central figure in Revelation, and perseverance as the theme. But claiming that someone is the protagonist or that something is the theme of a book is not the same as demonstrating that claim. In Revelation, grammatical-historical and literary analyses unite in their testimony that Christ is the central figure. Good literature uses a combination of description, "roundedness" or development, plot activity, and prominent location to demonstrate the primacy of one character over another. The book of Revelation follows this pattern. Jesus Christ receives the clearest descriptions, deepest development, most important plot activities, and most prominent locations of any character in the book. We cannot interpret the book correctly without looking for Him.

THE TITLES AND DESCRIPTIONS OF CHRIST

We identify ourselves by names and titles. Many CEOs make sure that everyone recognizes their position. We identify vice presidents, MDs, senators, principals, and managers by titles. Titles set us apart. We find the same to be true when we enter the biblical world. The breadth and diversity of titles and descriptions of Christ in Revelation set Him apart as a distinct and preeminent figure.

---

what the Old Testament says of Him. He will reign as King on the throne of David on earth in Jerusalem.

Titles Indicate Christ's Preeminence

Authors often indicate the superiority of one character over another and the centrality of a character by giving detailed descriptions of the prominent figures. If we read Revelation carefully through this lens, we discover that the other characters in the book are shallow, undeveloped or underdeveloped, and clearly secondary. Table 10 lists many of the secondary characters in the book with their attending titles. Compare this table with table 11 below for a visual impression of the supremacy of Christ. Where John applies no additional titles to a particular character (such as with the elders or the seven Spirits of God), the table below lists "none" in the column of titles.

Table 10—Secondary Characters & Their Titles in Revelation[2]

Character	Titles
God	Him which is, and which was, and which is to come (1:4; 1:8?; 4:8) Alpha and Omega (1:8?) The beginning and the ending (1:8?) The Lord (1:8?; 4:11) The Almighty (1:8?) + permutation Lord God Almighty (4:8) God (frequently)
John	A bond-servant (1:1) Your brother (1:9) Companion in tribulation, and in the kingdom and patience of Jesus Christ (1:9)
Seven spirits	None (1:4; 5:6)
Antipas	My faithful martyr (2:13)
A woman	Jezebel (2:20)
A strong angel	None (5:2)

[2] References followed by a question mark may actually be titles applied to Christ. For example, the titles in 1:8 may well refer not to the Father but to Christ.

Character	Titles
Elders	None (4:4, 10, etc.)
4 living things	None (4:6–8)
Colored horses	None (6:1–9)
Souls of the slain	None (6:9)
Kings of the earth	None (6:15). The verse adds great men, rich men, chief captains, mighty men, slaves, and free men, none of which refer back to the kings.
Four angels	None (7:1)
Another angel	None (7:2)
144,000 of Israel	Servants of our God (7:3)
Great multitude	None (7:9)
A fallen star	None (9:1)
King over the demonic locusts	The angel of the bottomless pit (9:11) Abaddon (9:11) Apollyon (9:11)
Locusts	None (9:3, etc.)
Two witnesses	Two olive trees (11:4) Two candlesticks (11:4)
Satan	Devil (2:10) Great red dragon (12:3) Dragon (12:4, etc.) The old serpent (12:9) Serpent (12:14)
Antichrist	Beast from the abyss (11:7) Beast from the sea (13:1) Beast (13:2, etc.) First beast (13:12)
False prophet	Another beast (13:11) False prophet (16:13, etc.)

TABLE 11—TITLES OF CHRIST IN REVELATION[3]

Title	Location
Almighty	1:8; 15:3; 16:7, 14; 19:15
Alpha and Omega	1:8; 22:13
Amen	3:14
Beginning and the End	22:13
Beginning of the creation of God	3:14
Christ	1:1, 2, 5; 11:15; 12:10; 20:4, 6
Faithful and True	19:11
Faithful Witness	1:5; 3:14
First and the Last	1:17; 2:8; 22:13
Firstborn from the dead	1:5
Holy One	3:7
Jesus	1:1, 2, 5, 9; 12:17; 14:12; 17:6; 19:10; 20:4; 22:16, 20, 21
King of kings	17:14; 19:16
King of saints	15:3?
Lamb	5:6, 8, 12, 13; 6:1, 16; 7:9, 10, 14, 17; 12:11; 13:8, etc.
Lion of the Tribe of Judah	5:5
The Living One	1:18
Lord	11:4,[4] 8; 14:13; 22:20, 21
Lord of lords	17:14; 19:16
One Who is, and Who was, and Who is coming	1:8?; 16:5?
One Who has His eyes as a flame of fire	2:18
One Who has the key of David	3:7

[3] An extensive discussion of the meaning of these titles can be found in commentary literature and is drawn together in Hand, *The Worthy Champion*, 105–16.

[4] The Byzantine Text type alternately supports either *Lord* or *God* in this location where the *Textus Receptus* uses *God*.

Title	Location
One Who has the seven spirits of God	3:1
One Who has the sharp double-edged sword	2:12
One Who holds the seven stars in His right hand	2:1
One Who opens and no one will shut	3:7
One Who searches the reins and hearts	2:23
One Who walks in the midst of seven candlesticks	2:1
Root of David	5:5; 22:16
Prince of the kings of the earth	1:5
Bright and Morning Star	22:16
Son of God	2:18
Son of man	1:13; 14:14?
The True One	3:7, 14; 19:11
The Word of God	19:13

The depth and frequency of Christological titles creates the strong impression that Christ is the central figure. He is preeminent. No other person or being comes close. Even comparing the titles for God the Father, the Holy Spirit, Satan, and Antichrist to those used of Christ indicates this strong emphasis on Christ's centrality.

Several important Old Testament titles for the Messiah imply that Israel has not lost the fulfillment of Old Testament prophecies by rejecting Christ at His first coming. For example, the "Root of David" (Rev. 5:5; 22:16) alludes decisively to Jeremiah 23:5–6, in which salvation and righteousness finally come to Israel and Judah through their Messiah:

> Behold, the days come, saith the Lord, that I will raise unto David a righteous Branch, and a King shall reign and prosper, and shall execute judgment and justice in the earth. In his days Judah shall be saved, and Israel shall dwell safely: and this is his name whereby he shall be called, The Lord Our Righteousness.

Jeremiah's prophecy alludes to the fact that Israel and Judah are unrighteous. Israel warrants God's judgment, but God will not cut her off because He has covenanted with the nation as His people. Revelation recalls to mind the expectation that national Israel finds its salvation in the Messiah. He will turn Israel toward righteousness. Thus Revelation alludes to Christ as One Who is capable of turning a wicked, rebellious nation into a righteous nation. This is exactly the hope of Old Testament prophecy. Revelation portrays Christ as Daniel's "Son of man."

> I saw in the night visions, and, behold, one like the Son of man came with the clouds of heaven, and came to the Ancient of days, and they brought him near before him. And there was given him dominion, and glory, and a kingdom, that all people, nations, and languages, should serve him: his dominion is an everlasting dominion, which shall not pass away, and his kingdom that which shall not be destroyed (Dan. 7:13–14).

This allusion is direct. Although Revelation does not join the title, Son of man, directly with Christ's receiving the kingdom as in Daniel, the title sets the stage for the entire book, in which Jesus Christ is receiving His earthly kingdom and subduing all nations and peoples before Him.

Several of the titles of Christ connect Him directly with God in the Old Testament. For example, "the first and the last" draws from Isaiah 44:6: "Thus saith the Lord the King of Israel, and his redeemer the Lord of hosts; I am the first, and I am the last; and beside me there is no God" (cf. Isa. 41:4; 48:12). A phrase very similar to Revelation's "King of kings" occurs in Nebuchadnezzar's praise in Daniel 2:47: "Of a truth it is, that your God is a God of gods, and a Lord of kings." In addition, Christ is the Almighty in Revelation, and He is "the mighty God" in Isaiah 9:6.

The reader senses the majesty of Christ as quality after quality and title after title describe His perfections, His character, and His power. Unlike the apocalyptic literature, Revelation is eminently Christ-centered.

Physical Descriptions Indicate Christ's Preeminence

Titles provide only part of the picture of Christ's glories in this book. If we chart the *physical* descriptions of the people in Revelation, a similar picture emerges. Revelation portrays reality through vivid images. The imagery serves as the vehicle for plot and emphasis. While Antichrist and other secondary figures receive some development in this realm (various horns, colors, and characteristics ascribed to them), they still fall far short of the descriptions of Christ (see table 12). Every other character in Revelation seems flat and undeveloped by comparison. We do not know much about John, about the people in the early churches, or about the people alive in the end of time, but a careful reading of Revelation leaves us with the knowledge of Christ. The description of His glorified state awes John and us. His power and authority are evident; His glory, unquestioned.

Table 12—Physical Descriptions of Jesus Christ in Revelation

Reference	Description
1:13–16	one like unto the Son of man
	clothed with a garment down to the foot
	girt about the paps with a golden girdle
	his head and his hairs were white like wool, as white as snow
	his eyes were as a flame of fire
	his feet like unto fine brass, as if they burned in a furnace
	his voice as the sound of many waters
	he had in his right hand seven stars
	out of his mouth went a sharp twoedged sword
	his countenance was as the sun shineth in his strength
5:6	a Lamb as it had been slain
	having seven horns and seven eyes
19:11–13	he that sat upon the white horse
	his eyes were as a flame of fire
	on his head were many crowns
	he had a name written, that no man knew, but he himself
	clothed with a vesture dipped in blood

Psychological Descriptions Indicate Christ's Preeminence

Revelation's description of the psychological states of its characters also singles out Christ as the most important character (see table 13 below). John exhibits fear/awe and extreme grief, but these emotional outbursts are rare. Beyond his emotional state, we know little of his psychological approval or disapproval of what he sees. Of course, we can presume that he approves of Christ's victory

(Rev. 22:20), but nothing in the plot line of Revelation gives us insight into his psychological makeup.

Fear never appears in Christ's psychological descriptions. He commands His people not to fear (Rev. 1:17; 2:10). Other characters fear the resurrection of the two witnesses (11:11). They fear God's name or His person (11:18; 14:7; 15:4; 19:5), and they fear the torment that falls on Babylon (18:10, 15), but the Lamb exhibits no fear.

A charting of what we would consider psychological qualities makes one quality stand out from all the others—God's wrath. Since the actions of the Father and of Christ are not always distinguishable in Revelation, the indications of wrath appear in the column listing Christ's qualities. Warrant for this decision stems from 6:16–17, in which "the face of him that sitteth on the throne, and . . . the wrath of the Lamb" and "their[5] wrath" appear together, as well as from 19:15, in which Christ is the active agent in the outworking of the "fierceness and wrath of Almighty God." These verses seem to indicate that Christ, not just the Father, is the wrathful One in view in Revelation. Christ is more than the agent of the Father's wrath; He is expressing His own wrath as well. Wrath has a disproportional representation in Revelation when compared to the rest of Scripture. Of eighteen instances of "wrath" (*thumos*; θυμός) in the New Testament, ten appear in Revelation (55% of the total). Of forty-five references to "anger" (*orgē*; ὀργή, ὀργίζω), eight occur in Revelation (18% of the total). Yet Revelation comprises only about five percent of the New Testament. In Revelation wrath dominates the other psychological states. Christ wages a just and vengeful war on His enemies.

[5] The stronger textual evidence favors "their" (αὐτῶν) over the KJV's "his" (αὐτοῦ), which is based on the *Textus Receptus*.

Table 13—Psychological Qualities in Revelation

Psychological Quality	Christ	All Other Characters
Faithfulness	1:5—f. witness 3:14—the f. and true witness 19:11—called F. and True	2:13—Antipas, my f. martyr 17:14—those with Christ are f.
Love	1:5—l. us and washed us 3:9—I have l. thee 3:19—as many as I l. I rebuke	2:4—church left its first l. 12:11—martyrs l. not own lives 22:15—wicked l. and make a lie
Hate	2:6—h. deeds of the Nicolaitans 2:15—h. deeds of the Nicolaitans	2:6—church h. deeds of Nicolaitans 17:16—10 horns h. the whore
Anger/wrath	6:16—w. of the Lamb 6:17—day of his w. has come 11:18—God's w. is come 14:8—w. of her fornication 14:10—w. of God 14:19—w. of God 15:1—w. of God 15:7—w. of God 16:1—w. of God 16:19—fierceness of his w. 18:3—w. of her fornication 19:15—fierceness and w. of Almighty God	12:12—devil has great w.

Christ also demonstrates a level of self-awareness or self-understanding that substantiates His place as the protagonist or main character in two ways. First, He possesses a greater self-awareness than other characters, and second, His self-awareness leads to His exercising inherent authority. Several other characters show us that they do not understand their rightful place in the scheme of things. John, for example, falls down twice in front of angels, attempting to worship them (19:10; 22:8–9). The context indicates that he does not grasp the similarity of function between angels and men (both are servants of God) or the radical distance between angels and God in majesty and worthiness of worship. John simply exhibits the behavior of a person who does not know how to act because he does not know his exact "place" in the relation to other beings. Similarly, the dragon shows a lack of self-awareness in his attempt to fight Christ in the first place (12:7–9, 12–17; 20:1–3, 7–10). If he knew his rightful place, the defectiveness of his power, and the derived quality of his authority, he could not fight as one deserving of this high place and one powerful enough to secure it. Finally, the beast exhibits a lack of self-awareness. What power he does possess comes from Satan (13:2–7). He thinks that he wields all power, that he can be like God, and that he can exterminate and make alive at will, but in reality even those whom he kills actually overcome him by the blood of the Lamb. Christ exposes the bankruptcy of the beast's self-confidence when He assaults the kingdom of the beast with darkness (16:10), when He uses dark powers to gather armies to their final destruction (16:14), and when He hurls the beast into the lake of fire (19:20).

In contrast to these other characters, Christ never misunderstands His Person, never overreaches His power, and never makes a misstep. He commands His churches by His own authority (2:5, 10, 16, etc.), He gives gifts by His own authority (2:7, 10, 17, etc.), He brings judgment by His own authority (5:2–5 cf. with ch. 6), He delegates power to others by His own authority (11:3), and He conquers by His own authority (19:11–21). On every hand the book exudes the fact that Christ knows exactly Who He is, and this fact contributes to our assessment that He is the central figure in Revelation.

A brief examination of the titles and descriptions of the characters in Revelation leaves us with the unavoidable impression that Jesus Christ is the focal character. The text provides more details about His appearance, His character, and His thinking than it provides about any other figure in the book. As we interpret this book, we must seek its message concerning Christ.

The Offices of Christ

The Scriptures present three basic offices that Christ fulfills—Prophet, Priest, and King. In fact, the various sections of the Old Testament demonstrate that human priests (the Pentateuch), human kings (the historical books), and human prophets (the prophetic books) cannot solve man's ultimate needs and deepest longings. These individuals may have been godly, but they could never lead the nation or even their own souls into the perfect realization of the covenants that God had made with Israel. The need for a perfect prophet, priest, and king went unmet until Christ came. While His first advent established His right, authority, and ability to be the expected Prophet, Priest, and King, it did not fulfill all that the Scriptures promised concerning these offices. Revelation closes the canon by portraying Christ in the crucial role of the immediate, literal, and rightful Prophet, Priest, and King.

Christ Our Perfect Prophet

Crucial passages in Revelation demonstrate that Christ is the very Word from the Lord that we need to hear and that He is simultaneously the Giver of that Word. Every other human prophet served as an intermediary between God and man, and nothing more. Christ is both the Intermediary of the Word of God and the immediate Word of God. Revelation demonstrates this in its opening verse:

> The Revelation of Jesus Christ, which God gave unto him, to shew unto his servants things which must shortly come to pass; and he sent and signified it by his angel unto his servant John.

Christ reveals this book to His servant John. The Father gave the revelation to Christ, and Christ stands in the role of the prophet. Yet He is no ordinary prophet. Other prophets spoke, "Thus saith the Lord." Jesus speaks "Thus saith I." In His address to each of the seven churches, He uses part of the description of Himself in chapter 1, coupled with that prophetic formula "thus saith" to indicate that He is Yahweh. He reveals perfectly the mind of God to man without an intermediary. This fact has practical implications for the content of the word. An example of these implications appears in Revelation 3:8, 10:

> I have set before thee an open door, and no man can shut it: for thou hast a little strength, and hast kept my word, and hast not denied my name. . . . Because thou hast kept the word of my patience, I also will keep thee from the hour of temptation, which shall come upon all the world, to try them that dwell upon the earth.

The prophets of old spoke in the name of the Lord, but they had no personal power to effect the promises that God gave to them to speak. Christ, as our perfect Prophet, asserts His own power to do and to effect as He wills. Those who keep His word receive the promise of His own direct intervention to keep them from the hour of tribulation. Jeremiah and Isaiah could not promise that. Daniel could not keep himself from captivity, let alone effect the security of others. But Christ is no ordinary prophet. He is the perfect Prophet—God and man. He can accomplish all of these things because the Word is not some abstract vocalization of information that is given to Him. Rather, "his name is called The Word of God" (Rev. 19:13).

Every other true prophet of mankind preached his ethical message without the power to help the people obey that message. Every other prophet proclaimed the future without the capacity to bring that future near, to finish the fulfillments, to wrap up this earthly age, and to breathe life into the true word by making the word come true. In Revelation, Christ does all of these things. He preaches to His churches and then secures their ability to obey. He proclaims these end events and then breaks the seals to initiate, guide, and produce the end. He is the Word of God speaking the Word of God.

Christ Our Perfect Priest

We cannot move far into Revelation before the priesthood of Christ confronts and comforts us. Revelation 1:5 bursts into praise, "Unto him that loved us, and washed us from our sins in his own blood." The Scriptures make very clear that "without [the] shedding of blood [there] is no remission" (Heb. 9:22). The priesthood of the Old Testament required repeated sacrifices from sinful priests for sinful people without ultimate efficacy. Christ's priesthood, so gloriously explained in Hebrews, finds similar expression in Revelation. His blood has "washed us from our sins." Yet Revelation implies that this act is long past, completed, and never needing repetition since the saints cry out,

> Thou art worthy to take the book, and to open the seals thereof: for thou wast slain, and hast redeemed us to God by thy blood out of every kindred, and tongue, and people, and nation (Rev. 5:9).

He lives, and redemption is complete. He stands ready to receive the worship and praise of His people, and perfect justice against sin has been attained. His priesthood extends beyond the nation of Israel to every kindred, tongue, people, and nation. His blood guarantees the salvation of His people since they "are written in the Lamb's book of life" (Rev. 21:27).

The question sometimes arises regarding how people are saved during the Tribulation. Revelation answers with the perfect priesthood of Christ. Believers "have washed their robes, and made them white in the blood of the Lamb" (Rev. 7:14) and "overcame [Satan] by the blood of the Lamb" (Rev. 12:11). His sacrifice applies backward and forward in time to all who believe in Him.

His priesthood also secures for His people certain guarantees for the future. Although He must have authority (kingship) to grant these blessings, He could not draw people into heaven without a priesthood that makes them clean. So when He grants people access to the tree of life (2:7), or when He gives a crown of life (2:10), when He clothes them in white garments (3:5) or makes them pillars in the temple of God (3:12), He attests that the blood of the Lamb in earlier and later chapters was effective in accomplishing what the blood of lambs could not. His priesthood is perfect.

One implied evidence of Christ's priesthood in Revelation derives from the access that the people have to Him personally. There seems to be no distancing of the redeemed from the Lamb. They stand in His presence. In fact, they stand in the presence of the One Who sits on the throne—a possibility almost inconceivable to us in our present state of sinfulness. The fact that believers stand in the presence of the Lamb means that He has not removed Himself from His people. The fact that the redeemed ones stand in the presence of God means that the sacrifice of the Lamb is superior to any conceivable sacrifice of animals. His blood is more excellent; His priesthood, perfect.

An additional feature demonstrates the priesthood of Christ. *Lamb* is the title most frequently used of Christ in Revelation. This fact strikes us as unusual since the book seems more oriented toward kingship. But His kingship and His priesthood are inseparable. He redeems a people and makes them His kingdom (1:6; 5:10). Christ offers nothing other than Himself up as a sacrifice to God for the sins of the people. That His one shedding of blood could redeem myriads attests the supremacy of His priesthood. That His one sacrifice could birth a kingdom of priests means He is like no other priest. The saints in heaven look back on the cross as the defining redemptive moment, and they also look at the Lamb as their visible, exalted Priest.

Christ Our Perfect King

The kingship of Christ stands out most clearly among His offices in Revelation. He exercises all facets of government: legislative, executive, and judicial. He provides security for His own people, and He wages war against His enemies. He conquers territory, puts down rebellion, drags the incorrigible away to judgment, warns the unruly, establishes justice, and brings peace and prosperity. He also receives the worship that is due a divine King.[6] Table 14 notes the instances of Christ's kingship that appear in Revelation. It then subdivides this authority into categories with which we are familiar. The chart helps illustrate the fact that Christ seldom appears overtly in the middle section of Revelation. Instead the Lamb delegates authority to angels, to His people, and even to His enemies in order to accomplish His will.[7] His authority permeates the book even where it appears indirectly.

[6] By depicting Christ as uniquely worthy of worship and by denying the legitimacy of creature worship, Revelation contends against the emperor worship that existed in John's day.

[7] A study of the active and passive forms of the verb *to give* (δίδωμι) demonstrates two important facts. Christ operates under His own authority and initiative, and the evil

Table 14—The Kingly Authority of Christ

Legislative Authority[8]
2:5—remember
2:16—repent
2:25—hold fast
2:26—I will give power over the nations
3:3—remember, repent, hold fast
3:19—be zealous, repent

Judicial Authority
2:4—I have somewhat against thee
2:14—I have a few things against thee
2:17—I will give a white stone
2:20—I have a few things against thee
2:23—I will give according to your works
3:2—I have not found thy works perfect
6:10—judging
19:11—in righteousness he doth judge
20:11–15—great white throne judgment

Executive Authority
1:5—prince of the kings of earth
1:6—dominion forever
1:7—cometh with the clouds
1:8—the Almighty
1:13—the Son of man
1:16—a sharp two-edged sword
1:18—keys of death and hell
2:1—holdeth the seven stars
2:5—I will remove thy candlestick
2:7—I will give to eat
2:12—sharp two-edged sword
2:16—I will make war
2:21—I gave her [time] to repent
2:23—I will kill
3:7—hath the key of David
3:9—make them worship
3:12—make him a pillar
3:12—write upon him the name of my God
3:21—sit with me on my throne
5:5—Lion of the tribe of Judah
5:5—the Root of David
5:5—hath prevailed
5:6—seven horns
5:10—made us kings
5:13—power forever
6:1–12—broke the seals
6:4—grants authority
6:16–17—wrath of the Lamb
7:17—midst of the throne
11:3—grants power to two witnesses to carry out activity
11:15—kingdom of our Lord and of his Christ
12:10—power of his Christ
19:11—he wages war (see the whole section 19:11–21)
20:4, 6—reigned with Christ
22:1, 3—throne of the Lamb
22:16—root and offspring of David

triumvirate (Satan, the first beast, and the false prophet) operate under derived authority. See Hand, *The Worthy Champion*, 138–41, for a thorough discussion of this phenomenon.

[8] The legislative actions of Jesus Christ pertain primarily to His right to command His people. None of the activities listed as legislative are exclusively legislative. They also involve His executive power and the threat of judicial action if people do not obey.

This kingship does not fade in the middle of the book, where Christ seldom appears. Although many events occur in the lengthy middle section of Revelation, developed actors do not appear (with the exception of the dragon/beast/false prophet counterfeits to the protagonist). The reader gets the distinct impression that these events are unfolding based on the actions of the well-developed character, Jesus Christ. His breaking of the seals in chapter 6 launches all of the succeeding events that crowd upon each other until He returns to the foreground in chapter 19. New events (judgments) occur, but the same agent (Christ) is responsible for producing those events. His commanding His servants and His delegating of authority pervade all parts of Revelation.

The centrality of the throne in the book of Revelation depicts the kingship of Christ. The word *throne* (*thronos*; θρόνος) occurs sixty-two times in the New Testament. Of these, forty-seven (76%) occur in Revelation. Satan's throne appears in 2:13 and 13:2. The throne of the beast has one reference in 16:10. Thrones of the elders appear in 4:4 and 11:16. The thrones of the saints going into the millennial kingdom appear in 20:4. The vast majority of references refer to the throne of God the Father, but several crucial passages demonstrate the kingship of Christ by equating His throne with that of the Father (3:21; 7:17; 22:1, 3) or by Christ's speaking unilaterally from His throne (21:5). Revelation depicts the equality of Christ's rule with the Father's rule and demonstrates Christ's universal kingship by these references.

Coherence of Offices

We do not derive our hope and comfort from any one of these offices of Christ working individually. Our hope rests in Christ's fulfillment of all His offices in concert. We do not have to choose between one who is capable of redeeming us or one who can give us security. We hope in One Whose perfections make Him the perfect Prophet, Priest, and King simultaneously.

Many passages link His offices. For instance, Revelation chapters 1 and 5 show the offices of Christ operating in concert. He reveals himself as Priest and King (ch. 1), and He rules precisely because He has redeemed a people (ch. 5). When we look at Revelation, we should expect to see the perfections of Christ.

Christology in Classic Terms

Revelation contributes to the cumulative case of Scripture for both the humanity and the deity of Christ. His humanity appears most clearly through the images of Him in chapters 1 and 19. Although John sees Christ's glorified body, that body is unmistakably human. Christ has the appearance of a man overall (1:13) with glorified characteristics (1:14–16). Jesus has a corporeal existence that allows Him to touch John (1:17). He later rides a horse (19:11), wears crowns (19:12) and a robe (19:13), and has a physical body (19:16).

At least four converging lines of evidence demonstrate His deity in Revelation. Christ shares some titles with God the Father. He carries out actions of deity. And He shares both a throne and worship with the Father. Both Christ and God are called the Almighty, the Alpha and Omega, the Beginning and the End, God, and Lord at various points. Since, according to the Old Testament, God will not give His glory to another, the dual ascription of these titles makes a clear claim for the deity of Christ. The actions of Christ correspond directly to those of the Father. Revelation 6:16–17 associates God and Christ in the same moment of wrathful judgment. Both serve as the temple of the new Jerusalem (21:22). Both illuminate that city (21:23). They share the same throne (22:1, 3), and they receive identical worship (5:13; also cf. 4:11 with 5:12). Revelation clearly presents Christ as having the same essence as the Father.

The Intersection of a Predominantly Literal Method and Christology

To the extent that we do not know the meaning of the book, we cannot draw Christological conclusions. If Revelation provides a predominantly symbolic perspective of the past-present-future (no one knows, since the symbolism is essentially inscrutable), we cannot make deductions concerning His actual glorified appearance, the nature of His kingship, or the types of His judgments. If we sever the text from a predominantly literal interpretation, the persons, events, and causations become so thoroughly muddled as to admit no clear Christology other than a general belief that somehow, somewhere, at some time He is ruling over somebody and bringing some kind of judgments against some group of bad people. Symbolic interpreters come to Revelation with certain presuppositions and are able to inject meaning where necessary to keep Revelation from being quite so pointless. But, in fact, the symbolic method reduces all such injection of meaning to speculation. The conservative symbolic interpreter can claim a high Christology, while the liberal can deny Christ. The preterist can claim a first-century Christological referent, while the historicist and idealist can claim a church-age Christological reference. None has more warrant than any other.

Symbolic interpretation of Revelation does real damage to truth by preventing us from discerning what Christ is revealing. If the book is symbolic, He is communicating through a vagueness and imprecision of terms that sound more like the pagan oracles than like the God Who knows the future (Isa. 46:10). Such communication diminishes the perfection of His prophetic office significantly since His prophecies are unclear, not particularly meaningful or necessary, and certainly less directly applicable than any prophecies in the rest of Scripture. Christ is a superior, not an inferior, prophet. His kingship is a decisively heavenly and earthly kingship, not an opaque or incomprehensibly veiled one. His priesthood is powerful enough to save both the church *and* Israel, as He promised in both Old and New Testaments. He is the Faithful and True Witness Who does not hide His testimony so darkly, couched in uncertain images, that it remains indecipherable today. He reveals in normal, predominantly literal communication the truth about Himself, about mankind, and about the future so that His people may know with clarity some of the plans that lie in the mind of God.

5

Revelation with a Purpose

The book of Revelation exists in God's plan for several clear purposes. God intends to convey a picture of the future through Revelation (1:1; 22:6). He also plans to edify His people through the book by giving them warning, encouragement, and blessing as appropriate to their faith and obedience (1:3; 16:15; 22:7, 14). He plans to accomplish these objectives through clear communication since vague, mythical, and uncertain images hardly clarify the future or edify people. Revelation has value for the people of God. Commitment to this assertion should appear through our study, reading, and proclamation of it within the church.

A Picture of the Future

Prophecy exists for numerous reasons, but one of the most important is the communication of future events in identifiable, verifiable terms.[1] Prophecy has ethical concerns, but the ethical teaching of prophecy depends on God's knowledge of the future and His communication of that knowledge to His people. In essence, God motivates us "in the now" by telling us what is coming in the future. If we had no conception of a coming judgment, we

[1] As a genre, prophecy is by nature less clear than history or epistle, but its clarity is adequate to recognize its accurate fulfillment and to avoid the charge of indecipherability. Layton Talbert lists twenty-two biblically defined reasons for the existence of prophecy, but he observes that foremost among these is "to provide understandable information and certain knowledge about future events" (unpublished lecture notes). He also notes, "God gives us information about the future . . . because He actually wants us to know what's going to happen."

would have no motivation to repent (2 Pet. 3:10–14). If we had no expectation of blessing, we would flee from the salvation that He offers.

It is the literalness and futurity of prophecy that undermines false teaching and adds credibility to the Bible's depiction of both physical and spiritual reality (Isa. 41:21–29). False teachers cannot predict the future as God can. They can offer vague symbols that could have any number of referents or fulfillments while God frequently speaks of specific nations, people, and events. By doing so, He proves Himself worthy of our confidence. He demonstrates that He is God and not a man.

At the same time, the futurity of prophecy allows the believer to exhibit his faith when he believes exactly what God asserts (Dan. 9:2–3). Previously fulfilled prophecies confirm that this faith is fully warranted. Scripture never scorns those who eagerly anticipated a coming, earthly Redeemer as narrow-minded, hyperliteral materialists (Luke 2:25–32). Rather, God blessed them for their faith. Simeon's faith provides particular instruction in this light. God promised Simeon that he would not die before seeing the Christ. Although thousands of Jews had waited hundreds of years for this moment, Simeon actually experienced it in exact, literal fulfillment of prophecy. He did not spiritualize the prophecy given to him as if he would experience some sort of vision of faith, and as he held the baby Jesus in his arms he cried out in praise for the literal fulfillment of God's prophecy.

The futurity of prophecy edifies us because it assures us that God has everything under His control. When we face catastrophe, the disintegration of our civilizations, the overthrow of nations, and the violent assault on our faith, we do not need a pat on the back and the glib generality, "It will all turn out all right in the end." We need the soul-stirring assurance from Almighty God that He has declared the end from the beginning (and has chosen to do so with a significant degree of specificity). Prophecy grounds our hope. It encourages faith with specific, God-given information about the future. When we see this world eagerly desiring a godless unity of commerce, political structures, and military might, we do not need to fear since Scripture has already told us that such a unity will come at some point. Yet we also know how Christ triumphs. The specific, literal promises of God provide a comfort that open-ended spiritualizations cannot.

The futurity and specificity of prophecy motivate intense prayer and repentance in God's people (Dan. 9:2–19) while distinguishing them from unbelievers, who do not repent (Heb. 11:7). The unbeliever laughs at prophecy as a vestige of an archaic religious mindset that has no basis in reality. The apocalyptic fervor that waxes in our own generation illustrates this attitude. People may believe that the world will perish from an asteroid, earthquake, terrorism, nuclear holocaust, or global warming or cooling, but they will not assent to its perishing at the hands of its King, Jesus Christ. The predictions in Revelation concerning specific plagues and events seem peculiar, even impossible, at times, but the past fulfillment of prophecy warrants our confidence in a future, literal fulfillment. The opponents of the literal fulfillment of prophecy have not fared well in the past. The people of Noah's generation thought him a fool for building a boat so far from water. Add to this the fact that flooding the entire earth was an absurd, unthinkable proposition, and we can understand why people might reject Noah's prophetic preaching. But the literality of his prophecy should have brought repentance to anyone willing to hear. All ignored and rejected it, but God brought the literal flood of waters upon the face of the whole world just as He had promised. Abraham, having received a prophecy that indicated Isaac was the promised seed, obeyed God's command to sacrifice him (Heb. 11:17–19). He had enough confidence in the literality of God's promise to know that God would fulfill the prophecy in spite of circumstance. Abraham did not know how God would fulfill the prophecy literally, but his faith was so strong that he believed that God could raise Isaac from the dead, if necessary (an absurdly unlikely event), in order to fulfill His promise. He did not spiritualize the "life" of Isaac or the promise of God.

Revelation portrays the future. It clearly indicates the rise of a powerful world ruler who demands the allegiance of all those under his dominion, who manipulates world economies to crush his enemies, and who derives his power from Satan. God will bring a series of judgments on the earth—one of which is the world ruler just mentioned—leading up to the Second Coming of Christ. Some of the judgments are entirely "natural" in their appearance (ch. 6). Others move into the supernatural (chs. 8–9, 16). All these earthly events will culminate in Christ's personal conquest of the armies gathered to fight Him (ch. 19) and the establishment of a one-thousand-year-long kingdom (ch. 20). At this point God creates a new heaven and new earth and brings His own dwelling down to man (chs. 21–22).

For His own purposes God has determined that this knowledge of the future will benefit His people. At very least, those who read and hear its prophecy (1:3) are blessed. The term *blessed* conveys the thought of happiness, but it is not the glib smile-on-the-face type of happiness. Rather, it is the enviable condition of possessing what everyone wants to possess. This condition involves but is not limited to a deep-seated peace, a quiet confidence, a settled security, a sure hope for the future, a guarantee that all will end well, a life of purpose, and a destiny of glory. Is it really surprising that a book like Revelation would bring this enviable condition to bear on those who know Christ? Reading it quiets the agitation of the Christian who fears the world in his own generation. Hearing it settles the heart by reminding us that God is in control, and that the Lamb Who died for us has not forgotten us or left us to fend for ourselves in a never-ending cycle of world empires. Studying it impresses us with the conviction that God never leaves loose ends. He will fulfill His promises to Israel in spite of every appearance to the contrary. We who know the Lamb, the King of kings, the Alpha and Omega, really are in an enviable condition. We will attain the security, the joy, the peace, the dominion, and the glory that earthly kings and rich men have sought for long ages of the earth. That Revelation speaks of the end of this earth age and the judgments that attend it should not confuse believers or cause them to cast it aside as irrelevant or unnecessary. It should create in us the desire to take it up and find the solace that God intends to provide for us from the darkness and fear that creeps across every generation.

A Plan for Edification

The practical consequence of its divine origin is that Revelation has immediate, significant value for us today. God intends a book like Revelation to test our faith, to separate between believers and unbelievers, to warn us about our sin, to provide the hope of blessing for the future, and to stabilize our souls against the "wisdom" of this world and the assaults of both false teachers and an evil culture.[2] He grants blessings to those who read His Word and take

---

[2] Even though her conclusion concerning an atemporal referent for Revelation is not warranted, Judith L. Kovacs correctly observes that "there is a depth and richness to Revelation that is lost when it is regarded simply as a blueprint for the future." "The

it seriously, to those who fix their hopes on His plan, and to those who carefully and diligently study how these things will come to pass. He secures and strengthens the faith of those who believe His prophecies. And He proves that He alone is God.

If we look for the great themes of Scripture in the book of Revelation, we begin to recognize that Revelation presents a witness that is entirely consistent with the other biblical books. The need to spiritualize its interpretation disappears when the reader pays adequate attention to the threads of doctrine that a normal reading of the book uncovers. Those who find Revelation a dry, pointless, and inscrutable book need to read more carefully. Those who cannot find doctrine in its plain words and insist on the need to interpret it symbolically need to look in it more carefully for the great themes of Scripture. Revelation exists to provide doctrine, reproof, correction, and instruction in righteousness, just as all the Scriptures do.

Edification does not derive from what we wish the text to say. True edification stems from the meaning of the text as God has given it. This position of humility causes the interpreter to recognize that God knows better than we what His church needs. We might think the church needs a short-term, immediate encouragement, when God knows that a long-term, distant-horizon encouragement is more important. In the attempt to make Revelation (and other prophecy) relevant to an immediate age, some interpreters actually destroy the God-ordained, more substantial relevance of the prophecy.[3] Neither Israel nor the church needs quick fixes. We

---

Revelation to John: Lessons from the History of the Book's Reception," *Word & World* 25, no. 3 (2005): 255.

[3] The first-century church did not really need to know that God was about to destroy Jerusalem in AD 70 or Rome in AD 476. It needed to know that history itself has a purpose and an end. What good would it have done the church to know that God would

need a covenant-making God to comfort us and to tell us that His promises have not been derailed by indicating that He not only knows the future but is orchestrating all events to produce His desired end. Myth is cold comfort. The naïve and childish hide in its balmy cloak oblivious to the devastating storm that approaches. Only truth provides real hope, and God has chosen to reveal truth about the future to His people.

The Theme of Christ

We have already seen the theme of Christ's Person in the previous chapter. Every facet of Christology edifies the believer. His power, His sacrifice, His redemption, His truth, His righteousness, and His victory produce in us the mixed emotions (fear, wonder, awe, sorrow for sin, joy) and the varied responses (faith, worship, obedience) that are consistent with our response to the doctrine of Christ elsewhere in Scripture.

The Theme of Election

Revelation reminds the reader that God stretches out the arm of His power to choose and redeem undeserving people for His own glory. This sovereign election appears decisively in Revelation 7. Israel, long disobedient to the law of God and long dismissive of her Messiah, experiences the inauguration of her salvation and beginning of her restoration during the Tribulation. Christians who have interpreted Scripture correctly have anticipated this event (Amos 9:11–15; Obad. 17–21; Mic. 5:2–15; 7:18–20; Zeph. 3:8–20; Rom. 11:1–2, 26).

---

destroy the Jews, who were persecuting the church, by the Romans, who would persecute the church infinitely more severely? What good would it have done the first-century church to know that over four hundred years distant God would destroy Rome but leave history itself an open question?

Absorbing into the church the promises that God gave to Israel may solve one difficulty, but it creates larger ones. If God is capable of supplanting literal, earthly promises to Israel with figurative, spiritual promises to the mystery church, then the church has no basis for its confidence in God's promises for its future. The church has acted as rebelliously, hatefully, and wickedly as Israel. One might respond that Christ's sacrifice guarantees that the promises to the church will come to pass. Granted. And His sacrifice guarantees that the promises to national Israel will come to pass as well. We might counter, "But there has always been a believing remnant even within a wicked visible church." Again, granted. But there has always been a believing Jewish remnant within the wicked nation of Israel. Moreover, the promises of God adhere to the nation of Israel in spite of Israel's sin, not because of her holiness. That is the point of God's sovereign election. The Old Testament prophets uniformly condemn Israel's persistent, present sin. They all point to imminent judgment on the basis of that sin. And yet they consistently point to a coming day when God Himself will radically transform His people's hearts so that they become His believing people, Israel. The biblical image of Israel is not merely a righteous Israel within national Israel, although that situation existed for a time, but a believing Israel made coextensive with national Israel by the power of God. Revelation edifies us as we observe the theme of His sovereign election. Nothing in human history can thwart God's purposes. Nothing can turn aside His promise. Nothing can reduce to shambles the powerful choice that He makes to redeem a people for His own glory:

> These shall make war with the Lamb, and the Lamb shall overcome them: for he is Lord of lords, and King of kings: and they that are with him are called, and chosen, and faithful (Rev. 17:14).

Several additional passages in Revelation communicate the theme of God's election. Revelation 13:8 says, "And all that dwell upon the earth shall worship him, whose names are not written in the book of life of the Lamb slain from the foundation of the world." The order of the Greek phrases leaves the referent of the phrase "from the foundation of the world" open ended. It may mean the "Lamb slain from the foundation of the world," or it could mean "written in the book of life from the foundation of the world." A later passage, Revelation 17:8, is not at all ambiguous. It specifically indicates, "whose names were not written in the book of life from the foundation of the world." Thomas Ice observes that in this verse "pretemporal election is taught in Revelation."[4] Revelation does not treat this election as an excuse for the unbeliever to remain in his sin, justifying himself as "non-elect" and incapable of doing anything about it. Rather, the book presents election as a comfort and encouragement to believers. Nothing, not the severest of persecutions or the most withering "evidences" of God-forsakenness (trials) can remove them from Christ's hand.

The Theme of Sanctification

Unlike the apocalypses, Revelation has a strongly ethical message. The Jewish and Christian apocalypses separated the world into two camps: "us" and "them." Everyone in the "us" category awaits glory, blessing, and honor. Everyone in the "them" category is doomed to torment. Everyone in the "us" category is hoping that those torments come soon upon those in the "them" category. Revelation presents a different picture. The letters to the seven churches preach a strongly ethical message to God's people (see table 15 below). The rebukes, warnings, and commands of

[4] Thomas D. Ice, "The Meaning of 'Earth Dwellers' in Revelation," *Bibliotheca Sacra* 166 (2009): 361.

Revelation 2–3 are substantially more like prophecy than apocalypse, especially since these chapters come directly from the mouth of the perfect Prophet, Jesus Christ. Many commentators have charted the letters and demonstrated the repeated appeals to repentance, the warnings against continuing in sin, the threats of impending judgment for failure to repent. These letters are to the "us" of the church since the church is not exempt from Christ's discipline. One should not read Revelation without sensing its immediate and urgent call for personal holiness and repentance where needed.

Table 15—Ethical Teaching in the Letters to the Seven Churches

Sin & Warning	Explicit Command	Blessing
2:4—left thy first love 2:5—I will remove thy candlestick	2:5—remember . . . repent . . . do the first works	2:7—eat of the tree of life
	2:10—do not fear suffering . . . be faithful unto death	2:10—a crown of life 2:11—not hurt by the second death
2:14—doctrine of Balaam 2:15—doctrine of the Nicolaitans 2:16—I will fight against them	2:16—repent	2:17—eat of the hidden manna . . . a white stone . . . a new name
2:20—permitting Jezebel to teach . . . permitting fornication 2:22—I will cast her into a bed . . . of great tribulation 2:23—I will kill her children	2:25—hold fast what you have	2:26–28—power over the nations . . . rule . . . morning star

Sin & Warning	Explicit Command	Blessing
3:2—I have not found your works perfect before God 3:3—I will come as a thief	3:2—be watchful, strengthen the things which remain 3:3—remember, hold fast, repent	3:4—walk with me in white 3:5—clothed in white, name not blotted out of the book of life, name confessed before God
	3:11—hold fast what you have	3:9—make enemies bow before you 3:10—keep you from the hour of temptation 3:12—make you a pillar in the temple of God, write on you the name of God, the name of Jerusalem, and my new name
3:15—neither cold nor hot 3:16—I will spew thee out 3:17—confident in your wealth 3:19—I rebuke and chasten	3:18—buy gold from me, white clothing, anoint thine eyes 3:19—be zealous, repent	3:21—sit with me on my throne

The plural *churches* in the refrain "He that hath an ear, let him hear what the Spirit saith unto the churches" (2:7, 11, 17, 29; 3:6, 13, 22) indicates that although these passages applied immediately to their original recipients, we who listen in on their rebuke and blessing have the opportunity to correct similar sins and shortcomings as well. Through these letters and through the book as a whole, Christ calls His people to a holy life. The white clothing that appears frequently in Revelation (3:4–5, 18; 4:4; 6:11; 7:9, 13–14; 19:8, 14) finds its explanation in Revelation 19:8:

> And to her was granted that she should be arrayed in fine linen, clean and white: for the fine linen is the righteousness of saints.

Revelation calls believers to a holy life. It insists that those who are the Lamb's own people are distinct from the world in their righteous conduct. Revelation does not leave the reader with the impression that a merely external membership in a visible group is adequate for eternal life. Holiness is requisite. Yet all our righteousness rests on Christ Himself:

> These are they which came out of great tribulation, and have washed their robes, and made them white in the blood of the Lamb (Rev. 7:14).

The Theme of Repentance

Unlike the apocalypses, Revelation does not present its readers as a closed group. In fact, the book indicates quite the opposite. Myriads of people will trust Christ in the Tribulation (7:9–14). Many of those will suffer martyrdom at the command of Antichrist (13:7–10). At some point the people of the earth make a conscious choice to accept Antichrist as their god and receive his mark (13:16). But until that time, the implicit warnings that come from the slow crescendo of judgments provide opportunity for repentance. Revelation clearly indicates that the people of the earth understand that Christ is judging their sin (6:16–17). Instead of gladly taking up God's offer, much of this world despises God and persists in sin:

> And the rest of the men which were not killed by these plagues yet repented not of the works of their hands, that they should not worship devils, and idols of gold, and silver, and brass, and stone, and of wood: which neither can

> see, nor hear, nor walk: neither repented they of their murders, nor of their sorceries, nor of their fornication, nor of their thefts (Rev. 9:20–21).
>
> And men were scorched with great heat, and blasphemed the name of God, which hath power over these plagues: and they repented not to give him glory. And the fifth angel poured out his vial upon the seat of the beast; and his kingdom was full of darkness; and they gnawed their tongues for pain, and blasphemed the God of heaven because of their pains and their sores, and repented not of their deeds (Rev. 16:9–11).

Additionally, there is a point in Revelation at which the majority of God's witnesses to faith have suffered martyrdom at the hands of the beast. Revelation 14:1 places the 144,000 of Israel in heaven, presumably having been destroyed by Antichrist since they were marked out on earth in chapter 7. Even at this point God extends the offer of repentance to humanity, and this time that offer arrives supernaturally. Revelation 14:6–7 says,

> And I saw another angel fly in the midst of heaven, having the everlasting gospel to preach unto them that dwell on the earth, and to every nation, and kindred, and tongue, and people, saying with a loud voice, Fear God, and give glory to him; for the hour of his judgment is come: and worship him that made heaven, and earth, and the sea, and the fountains of waters.

In this dark hour, when mankind has already sided with Antichrist to destroy God's people, when men have conspired to remove the witness against their sins from their presence, God sends a supernatural witness to offer hope and salvation to those who will

as proportional and perfectly fitting the crimes of mankind (16:5–7).[5] When the believer grasps the fact that God's justice is neither cruel nor hasty, neither slow nor forgotten, he experiences the edifying intent of this book. Revelation edifies the believer who reads it naturally and recognizes in it a vindication of the character of God.

The Theme of Victory

Victory permeates Revelation. From the individual victory of the believer to the final victory of Christ, the theme resounds throughout the book. This is no mere poetic license. Out of twenty-eight occurrences in the New Testament of the verb meaning "to overcome, to conquer" (*nikaō*, νικάω), seventeen occur in Revelation (61%). Most of these occur in the letters to the seven churches, where the believer overcomes in the sense of his salvation:

> To him that overcometh will I give to eat of the tree of life, which is in the midst of the paradise of God (2:7).
>
> He that overcometh shall not be hurt of the second death (2:11).
>
> To him that overcometh will I give to eat of the hidden manna, and will give him a white stone, and in the stone a new name written, which no man knoweth saving he that receiveth it (2:17).
>
> He that overcometh, and keepeth my works unto the end, to him will I give power over the nations (2:26).
>
> He that overcometh, the same shall be clothed in white raiment; and I will not blot out his name out of the book

[5] These verses provide a perfect example of divine *lex talionis*, the law of retribution.

> of life, but I will confess his name before my Father, and before his angels (3:5).
>
> Him that overcometh will I make a pillar in the temple of my God, and he shall go no more out: and I will write upon him the name of my God, and the name of the city of my God, which is new Jerusalem, which cometh down out of heaven from my God: and I will write upon him my new name (3:12).
>
> To him that overcometh will I grant to sit with me in my throne, even as I also overcame, and am set down with my Father in his throne (3:21).

Two instances apply directly to Christ and His victory:

> Weep not: behold, the Lion of the tribe of Juda, the Root of David, hath prevailed to open the book, and to loose the seven seals thereof (5:5).
>
> These shall make war with the Lamb, and the Lamb shall overcome them: for he is Lord of lords, and King of kings (17:14).

Additional instances include the beast's overpowering the world (6:2), the two witnesses (11:7), and tribulation saints (13:7). But these conquests are short-lived. In reality, the saints overcome the beast, even though they lose their lives (12:11; 15:2; 21:7).

Similarly, of twenty-five references to war or making war in the New Testament (*polem-*, πόλεμος, πολεμέω) fifteen occur in Revelation (60%). Although most of these passages cite the beast and his armies making war on the saints and on Christ, two indicate Christ is the warrior:

> I will come unto thee quickly, and will fight against them with the sword of my mouth (2:16).
>
> And I saw heaven opened, and behold a white horse; and he that sat upon him was called Faithful and True, and in righteousness he doth judge and make war (19:11).

These verses lead the reader to the conclusion that although victory seems securely in the grasp of earthly powers and the Antichrist, all such victory is transient. It yields itself up to the enduring, eternal victory of believers and the Lamb. The consolation that stems from these facts should be apparent to every believer. We do not seem to be "the mighty," "the powerful," "the wealthy," or "the victorious" in this present age, but we have divine assurance that this world is out of joint. Christ will reverse our apparent weakness and this world's apparent strength to reveal His own victory and our victory through Him. Even in this victory the necessity of normal interpretation appears. If Revelation speaks primarily in myth, symbol, and abstraction, then it has very little comfort to offer the believer. When a myth is recognized as a myth, it cannot offer genuine hope to its reader. Of course, if he understands a myth to be reality, he will derive comfort from its misunderstood "reality," but in this case his comfort is unwarranted.[6] Only a normally expressed, correctly understood promise of victory can provide a warranted comfort. Revelation edifies the believer by revealing actual events that lie in the future of this earth. The world is under

[6] Propaganda regularly capitalizes on this phenomenon. Causing its readers/hearers to believe an untruth, propaganda gives people a sense of power, victory, and comfort that is unwarranted. This occurred to great effect in World War II. The Germans and Japanese fed their people a modern myth of their invincibility and military successes. This practice led to a sense of well-being and comfort that was out of step with reality. The Jewish apocalypses were forms of propaganda. Is Revelation? Is it designed to give its reader a false sense of hope, victory, and comfort through grandiose images that have no grounding in reality? This hardly does justice to the nature of biblical revelation. God provides His people with real hope, not an illusion or mirage of hope.

the dominion of Christ. He will win not merely the spiritual battle that extends salvation to the soul but also the physical battle that reclaims the earth as His own territory and His own kingdom.

Summary

Revelation has value for the believer. God did not give us this book to confuse us or misdirect us. He also did not intend for us to use it as merely a book of facts or a series of images. We must read it carefully to discern what it teaches (its meaning) and what its teaching means for us today (its application). In this way Revelation will grant to us the blessing that God promised it would give to those who read it (1:3).

AN INTENTION OF CLARITY

God intends to communicate truth clearly to His people. There would be no need for Scripture if it merely hid the truth in esoteric terms. We should expect to find a reasonable degree of clarity in every book of the Bible, and Revelation exhibits that clarity both in its content and in its ordering.

Clarity in Content

God indicates both the purpose and content of the book of Revelation. He tells the readers that Revelation communicates the future: "The Revelation of Jesus Christ, which God gave unto him, to show unto his servants things which must shortly come to pass" (Rev. 1:1).[7] This verse answers questions concerning why and what God intends to accomplish with the book of Revelation. Christ

[7] Layton Talbert observes, "The only way prophecy can meaningfully affect the present is if its communication of that future is understandable. If we really can't be sure what such predictions mean, how can they have any meaningful impact on how we live? That would seem to reduce the ethical impact to something like, 'Be ye holy, because it seems that some really amazing things we don't really understand are going to happen one day'" (unpublished lecture notes).

gives these visions to John for the purpose of revealing information visibly ("to show"). Although Christ presented the book of Revelation to John in images, the medium does not contradict the literal quality of the book since the images that John experienced were accurate reflections of future reality. Verse 1 indicates that Revelation unveils the future.[8]

That Revelation requires some type of futurism, then, is not simply a logical deduction but a biblical necessity. None of the interpretive systems put Revelation's content in the past (from the standpoint of John's authorship). All acknowledge the clarity and literal meaning of this opening verse.[9] This seems to set the stage for the remainder of the book. If God intends to communicate at all, He must do so with adequate clarity, using normal rules of language, using comprehensible language and a predominantly literal thought flow. Otherwise, Revelation hides the very content that it ostensibly reveals.

Many interpreters confuse the fact that prophecy does not reveal *how* or *when* God will accomplish His Word with the fact that prophecy reveals *what* He plans to accomplish. This results in a muddying of interpretive waters by the unnecessary introduction of supposed symbols. Correctly recognizing that Revelation does not tell us *how* these creatures from the abyss (9:1–11) came into being, how they can torment people for so long without people's dying, and how they can look like locusts while possessing such diabolical characteristics, many interpreters abandon *what* the

---

[8] See "The 'Soon-' and 'Near-'ness of Revelation" in chapter 2 above for the proper contextual interpretation of "things which shall shortly come to pass" as a communication of imminent, not immediate, events.

[9] In fact, some systems treat only this verse and a couple of other verses literally at all. As noted in chapter 2, Preterism takes a narrowly literal (*not* the same thing as hyperliteral) interpretation of ἐν τάχει to arrive at its insistence for a first-century fulfillment.

text says, namely, that some type of literal but unfamiliar being comes up from the abyss and torments unregenerate mankind for a five-month period in the future as a direct divine reprisal against human sin. Correctly recognizing that Revelation does not tell us *how* God will raise the believing dead and seat them on earthly thrones, many interpreters deny what the text says, namely, that Christ will raise the bodies of His dead saints and reign with them for one thousand literal years.

Charges against futurism often center on those futurists who have departed from the *what* of Revelation into speculation on the *how* or *when* of the events. In my estimation, such critiques are necessary and appropriate. God has not called us to speculation. Even the futurist's imagination can run wild and cause him to abandon a predominantly literal interpretation in favor of date-setting and drawing immediate connections with current events. The fact that he, too, can err in positing a specific *how* and *when* God will act does not undermine the fact that Revelation tells us *what* God will do. Revelation becomes abundantly clear when the reader stops trying to figure out what God has *not* said and starts paying attention to what He *has* said. A literal method of interpretation, applied correctly, treats the content of the book seriously without resorting to wild speculation or the highly subjective interpretations of the other systems. Revelation is essentially clear.

Clarity in Order

People have broken down the organization of Revelation into several basic patterns.[10] Some interpreters believe that the book follows a chiasm, making the most important part of the book somewhere around chapter 12. Others think the book repeats the

[10] See Hand, *The Worthy Champion*, 158–72, for a much fuller treatment of these structures, their strengths and weaknesses, and their theological implications.

same basic era over and over again. This theory of recapitulation typically asserts that the book covers the entire church age seven times within the book of Revelation. In each cycle, the images become stronger, but the events are essentially the same.

Significant problems exist with both of these organizational patterns. No evidence for a chiasm exists outside of the introduction and conclusion of the book (chs. 1 and 22). Every proposed chiastic structure is haphazard and strained. None address the text very well, leaving the reader with the impression that the interpreter imposed the chiasm on the text from his own imagination. Recapitulation fares a little better, but it either forces contradictory events to occur simultaneously (silence in 8:1 and noise in 11:15) or claims that the individual seals, bowls, and trumpets do not match up directly at all. This would vitiate one of the primary arguments for recapitulation (the parallelism of lightning, thunder, and earthquake that appears in 6:12; 8:5; 11:19; and 16:18).

The convolutions that chiasm and recapitulation introduce into the text can leave the reader with the impression that these structures rely more on their need to prove a theological point than their obviousness from the context. For example, although a normal interpretation accepts Revelation's placement of the Second Coming (ch. 19) before the Millennium (ch. 20), those who dismiss the premillennial return of Christ *must find another organizational pattern* in Revelation in order to do away with the obvious implications. There is no textual break between 19:21 and 20:1 that could warrant the beginning of a new cycle of visions.

A more natural order admits an essentially linear progression that explains the increasing severity of judgment throughout the book. There are interruptions in the sequence (chs. 7, 10, 14–15), and there are flashbacks (ch. 12) as well, but both of these types of interruption fit better within a chronological framework than in chiasm or recapitulation. An essentially linear pattern observes that the church appears only in chapters 2 and 3. It does not appear overtly during the time of the Tribulation.[11] Chronological progression indicates that Christ will bring increasingly severe judgments on the earth and its wicked inhabitants leading up to His Second Coming.

Several structural patterns clearly occur in Revelation. Table 16 displays these structures. The phrase "in Spirit" (1:10; 4:2; 17:3; 21:10) occurs four times and seems to divide Revelation into four major sections. The expression "Write the things which thou hast seen, and the things which are, and the things which shall be hereafter" (1:19) implies a temporal division in the book. Revelation 4:1–2 links both of these expressions to indicate that the material following this point is both future in reference to time and new in reference to topic. Within the first of the three future sections, various sequences of seven provide additional structure. When the reader combines these sets of structure, he finds a carefully constructed structural outline of the book. Well-constructed literary structure does not indicate a symbolic meaning any more than God's creation in seven days would indicate mythical/symbolic meaning. God revealed to John His intentions concerning the future in a fashion that indicates God's character as being orderly and precise.[12]

---

[11] Those interpreters whose ecclesiology drives their eschatology turn all of the following into the church: the 4 beasts, the 12 elders, the 144,000 of the twelve tribes, the innumerable multitude, the saints under the altar, the two witnesses, the woman clothed with the sun, and the New Jerusalem. Since Christ has already addressed His churches explicitly by location, faults, merits, and promises, no adequate warrant exists for the assumption that He suddenly switches to symbols in reference to the church.

[12] Mathematics acknowledges the supreme order and organization in the creation, even while some theologians turn every such indication of order into a symbol. The

Table 16—Combined Structures in Revelation

Time	Topic	Enumerated Events	Other Elements
Past 1:9–20	Church 1:9–3:22		
Present 2:1–3:22			
Future 4:1–22:5	Conflict 4:1–16:21		
		7 seals 6:1–8:1	
			Sealing of servants ch. 7
		7 trumpets 8:1–15:8	
			7 thunders ch. 10
			2 witnesses ch. 11
			2 signs ch. 12
			2 beasts ch. 13
			Ethical comments ch. 14
			Heavenly tabernacle; shift to bowls ch. 15
		7 bowls 15:1–16:21	
	Conquest 17:1–21:8		
			Ruin of religious Babylon ch. 17
			Ruin of economic Babylon ch. 18
			Second Coming of Christ; ruin of Antichrist ch. 19
			Millennium ch. 20
			New creation 21:1–8
	Eternity 21:9–22:5		
			New Jerusalem 21:9–27
			New conditions 22:1–5

Each column shift to the right breaks Revelation down into successively greater detail. The first three columns present a higher order of structural attachment to the text (John makes quite clear that these sections are directly intended), while the fourth column adds

fractals observed by Benoît Mandelbrot, for example, remind creationists that God is supremely rational and orderly.

so many explanatory details that it offers little additional structure. The severing of the book at 4:1–2 indicates that the book does not recapitulate the same events in 1:9–3:22 and 4:1–22:5. The radical difference in topic, location, content, and form indicate that Eternity (21:9–22:5) cannot recapitulate the two middle sections, Conflict (4:1–16:21) and Conquest (17:1–21:8). So recapitulation tries to build its case based on tenuous connections among the enumerated sequences as well as in the undisputed fact that some of the explanatory elements use the technique of flashback to address the birth of Christ (ch. 12).

An essentially chronological understanding of Revelation fits the macrostructural elements very well. Past precedes present, which in turn precedes the future. The church age precedes Christ's first judgments against the world, which precede His final conquest of the world, which precedes eternity. There is nothing unnatural in this sequence. And while a chronological understanding must grapple seriously with the other structural elements, it assesses these structural pieces as natural literary devices such as foreshadowing, flashback, and explaining (zooming in on) specific details. Thus an essentially chronological understanding of Revelation has the following arguments in its favor. First, it follows the most natural order of literary works. Second, it explains the macrostructural elements of Revelation better than recapitulation and chiasm. Third, it creates the fewest difficulties while answering the most problems concerning structure. And fourth, it requires the least theological nuancing and special pleading to obtain its results.

Summary

The further the church moves toward a spiritual-symbolic understanding of Revelation, the less clear the book becomes. Both divine intent and divinely inspired structure point in the direction of greater rather than lesser clarity. Approaching Revelation with an awareness of its compositional clarity helps us read with the confidence that this book is intelligible and has significant value for God's people.

Interpretive Principles

If we could summarize the most basic interpretive principles that we ought to apply to Revelation, they would include the following.

First, *read Revelation as an intelligible book* given by a God Who wants His people to understand important issues about the future. We must not treat the book as if it were inscrutable.

Second, *read Revelation as a normal book.* We have to know grammar, vocabulary, logic, background history, and figures of speech to understand any meaningful book.[13] The same applies to the biblical books.

Third, *read Revelation with humility.* We should not try to predict events when God has not spoken, nor should we deny what He has spoken. He has not told us when or how these events will unfold, but He has told us that they will occur. We should not assume that we can piece together a perfect road map of the future, nor should we shy away from the road map that God has already provided. Either extreme tends toward an intellectual pride—the former in convincing one that he has the exact date, time, places, and persons figured out, and the latter in convincing one that the book is so esoteric that only spiritual elites can figure it out.

Fourth, *read Revelation as a testimony about* Christ. Scripture reveals the second person of the Trinity (Luke 24:26–27; John 5:39;

[13] This is simply grammatical-historical exegesis.

1 Pet. 1:10–12). God's Word focuses on our Savior. Look for Him. Magnify Him. Rejoice in His victory in this book just as much as you rejoice in His victory at the cross. Without the cross, Revelation would not be possible. Without Revelation, the cross would be under-realized and therefore defective. The future is not an end unto itself. We learn about it so that we can glorify God in Christ.

Fifth, *read Revelation as a practical book*. Revelation has immediate value for all of our lives. Interpretation (what it means) differs from application (what import it has for us), but application must occur. Revelation is for the church by the Lord of the church. We dare not write it off as uselessly complex or pointlessly vague. God, in Christ, through Revelation calls His church to knowledge of the future, to repentance of sin, to confidence in hope, to affirmation of His covenant promises, and to courage in a dark age. Nothing in the book is wasted. Nothing is superfluous. Scripture does not exist for the sake of drama alone. Revelation is for you.

Conclusion

We have surveyed crucial issues for understanding the Revelation of Jesus Christ. Observing the claims of Scripture about itself and the principles of language in general, we have drawn the following conclusions:

- A predominantly literal interpretation of prophecy has historical, biblical, and explanatory warrant for its insistence on a consistent interpretation method.
- Of the major systems of interpretation, futurism follows the literal interpretation of Scripture most closely, has the fewest anomalies, and exhibits the greatest explanatory power.
- Once the interpreter accepts a predominantly literal method and a futurist position, Premillennialism follows as a necessary conclusion. It also has independent biblical warrant.
- Revelation exists to teach us about the future, but these future events point us to Christ, rather than to themselves, as the ultimate focal point.
- God gave us this book to teach us, to rebuke us, to correct us, and to help us do what is right. Revelation is for the people of God. Its images, while difficult at times, are not opaque.

No book can cover every facet of theology, answer every contrary assertion, or advance every argument in favor of a particular position. But this book has provided guidance for defending a literal, futurist, premillennial position and for interpreting the book of

Revelation consistently and biblically. It also makes advances in discussions about the Christology of Revelation and the recognition of symbols.

Whether you concur with or critique this book, you should find Revelation a deep well of truth that is eminently applicable, personally edifying, and theologically valuable for God's people in every generation.

Appendix 1: Symbolic Interpretation—Its Argument, Weaknesses, and Refutation

The material in this appendix is the most complex argumentation in the book, but it provides a powerful warrant for the preceding argument. Until the interpreter settles in his mind the foundational questions of hermeneutics, he cannot proceed in his exegesis of a text. *Is Revelation symbolic or literal?* constitutes the single most important interpretive question. Interpreters have presented a number of arguments for symbolic interpretation, and this appendix addresses the more prominent of these, including church history, genre, word definitions, a desire for relevance, and the New Testament's use of the Old Testament.

The Historical Argument for Symbolic Interpretation

As we noted in chapter 1, church history shows us that literal interpretation was the earliest method of the church, while symbolic interpretation was the majority. Since symbolic interpreters often reference history as evidence for their system, a little historical background allows us to assess the merit of their claims.

The Alexandrian School[1]

The initial arguments in favor of symbolic interpretation derive from a third-century rejection of millenarian thought. The

[1] Numerous works serve as the basis for the following sections. Especially valuable resources include Lectures III and IV in Frederick W. Farrar, *History of Interpretation* (Grand Rapids: Baker Book House, 1961); and the chapters by R. P. C. Hanson, M. F.

Alexandrian school of interpretation, centered on Clement, Origen, and Dionysius, departed from a literal interpretation of the Scriptures in favor of an allegorical method.[2] In order to make Christianity more acceptable to their culture, the Alexandrian Fathers began integrating Platonic thought and Scripture. Reconciling Greek philosophy and Scripture required a non-literal method since pagan philosophy had little in common with the truths of divine revelation. At first, these writers allegorized anything that they considered irreverent, absurd, or impossible, but allegorical interpretation soon spread to the rest of Scripture. Since prophecies that were not fulfilled in Christ's first advent created a serious inconvenience for the church, these prophecies received the same spiritualizing treatment. Although later church fathers repudiated many of the excesses of the Alexandrian church and rejected its aberrant theological conclusions, the symbolic interpretation of prophecy took hold, multiplied, and became the predominant method.

Anti-Chiliasm and Anti-Judaism

Several church fathers indicate their personal distaste for the notion of a coming, earthly kingdom.[3] Some later fathers found the belief in a literal millennial kingdom too materialistic. Their rejection of chiliasm (the belief in the Millennium) required a symbolic interpretation of Revelation.

Wiles, and Gerald Bonner in *From Beginnings to Jerome*, vol. 1 of *The Cambridge History of the Bible*, ed. P. R. Ackroyd and C. F. Evans (Cambridge: Cambridge University Press, 1976).

[2] The antipathy of Dionysius to Revelation was so profound that he rejected John's authorship of Revelation, denied the imminent return of Christ and a literal, earthly kingdom, and slowed Revelation's acceptance into the canon in Alexandria.

[3] The writings of Eusebius provide a classic example. Eusebius attacked other church fathers as ignorant for holding premillennial views (*Ecclesiastical History*, III.39.12–13).

A few church fathers despised the Jews for their part in the crucifixion of Jesus and wanted no promises left for Israel's future. Since Scripture guarantees a revived Jewish kingdom with Christ as its King, the church created a symbolic method to reinterpret prophecy and to remove its application to Israel. This symbolic method passed from the fathers into the dogma of the Roman Catholic Church in the Middle Ages.

Symbolism prevailed from the third century onward for a number of reasons. It alleviated inconvenient prophecies concerning Israel. It fit current theological systems and justified existing presuppositions. And it provided intellectual satisfaction since only the scholarly elite could understand the symbols and mystic meanings of Scripture.

Present symbolic interpretation builds on these concepts of the past, but it does not remain slavishly devoted to them. From the time of the Reformation, interpreters have recognized the need to study the Scriptures independently of church dogma. Today when interpreters argue in favor of interpreting Revelation symbolically, they typically build their cases on certain features in the text and history.

Assessment of the Historical Argument

The historical argument cannot warrant symbolic interpretation. As a method of interpretation, symbolism did not arise from sound exegesis and biblical reasoning. It arose from the intrusion of Greek philosophy and theological prejudice into Scripture interpretation.[4]

---

[4] Pentecost, 23–24.

The symbolic interpretation of prophecy won by default once it carried over into the Roman Catholic Church. The amillennial doctrine of the Catholic Church requires a non-literal approach to Revelation; so the church propagated and defended what was consistent with its teachings. In a later generation, the Reformers spent most of their time on soteriology and ecclesiology rather than on eschatology. Where they did comment on eschatology, their remarks sometimes reflect negatively on their judgment. For example, in his *Preface to the Revelation of St. John* (1522 and 1527), Martin Luther wrote, "[I] consider it to be neither apostolic nor prophetic. . . . this is reason enough not to think highly of it: Christ is neither taught nor known in it."[5] Regardless of Luther's assessment, the kingship of Christ permeates the book. Although Calvin's commentaries cover the majority of Scripture, he wrote no commentary on Revelation. The meager record left by the Reformers does not warrant applying a symbolic method of interpretation.

THE GENRE ARGUMENT—REVELATION AS APOCALYPSE

Since the mid-1800s the notion of Revelation as an apocalypse has gained ground significantly in biblical studies. What modern scholars call *apocalyptic literature* arose in Judea in the intertestamental period. The era of the prophets had ended, and the Jews faced a sustained social and religious assault from their Greek masters, which eroded their hopes and which did not fit the Jews' prophetic expectations. The writers of apocalypses entered into this cultural situation. They did not claim inspiration as the prophets before them, but they tried to address the threat of cultural absorption by reporting dramatic visions of hope and deliverance. The Jewish apocalypses explain how the appearances of catastrophe on

[5] http://www.bible-researcher.com/antilegomena.html; accessed 26 August 2011.

earth do not match heavenly realities. They assert that judgment will destroy the wicked and save the righteous in the end. Since this type of literature arose after the collapse of Alexander's empire, scholars typically date the genre from 200 BC to AD 150. In fact, the recognition that Ezekiel, Daniel, and portions of Zechariah seem to match the apocalyptic genre led to an increasing attack on the conservative dates of these books by liberal writers.[6] The argument is that if they are apocalypses, they could not have appeared before 200 BC; and if they appeared before 200 BC, as the biblical books claim, they cannot be apocalypses.[7]

Several features of the apocalypses stand out due to their relevance for the interpretation of Revelation. Apocalyptic literature is visionary (revealed through visions), mediated by angels, and heavily symbolic. Writers who accept Revelation as an apocalypse gravitate naturally toward a symbolic interpretation of it.[8] Likewise, writers who hope for vindication of the symbolic method assume that it is an apocalypse. That a predominantly symbolic method applies at least to extra-canonical apocalypses is self-evident since none of the non-canonical apocalypses address literal future events. The writers of the apocalypses had no divine input and could not accurately depict the world to come.

---

[6] See for example John W. Bailey's grouping of Daniel with other writings of the Maccabean era in "Jewish Apocalyptic Literature," *The Biblical World* 25 (January 1905): 33.

[7] Hypothesizing some proto-apocalyptic genre is an unnecessary expedient. These Old Testament books are simply works of prophecy.

[8] Interpreters do not always recognize the contradictions that they introduce. Defending Revelation as an apocalypse in order to spiritualize the book requires that the interpreter accept the other features of apocalypse, one of which includes a distant eschatological salvation and distant supernatural world rather than an immediate salvation in the present world. Preterism, Historicism, Idealism, Postmillennialism, and Amillennialism want the symbolic interpretation, but they would prefer it without the baggage of a future eschatological salvation and a fixation on a distant supernatural world. Robert L. Webb, "'Apocalyptic': Observations on a Slippery Term," *Journal of Near Eastern Studies* 49, no. 2 (April 1990): 123.

Assessment of the Genre Argument

The designation of Revelation as an apocalypse is one of the wedges that the symbolic method uses to destroy the literal interpretation of Revelation, but the viability of that very wedge is in question. Symbolic interpreters assume what they have not proven. They wrongly believe that the designation of Revelation as an apocalypse is inviolable, but significant difficulties attend this claim.

Defining Apocalypse

Scholars struggle to define and describe what constitutes an apocalypse.[9] Leon Morris observes, "There is no consensus as to exactly what the term [*apocalypse*] denotes. There is no agreed list of apocalyptic books and it is not easy to define what we mean by apocalyptic literature."[10] In some cases a proposed definition is so broad as to include most Old Testament prophetic books. In others it is so narrow that it clearly excludes the book of Revelation. This means that scholars simply assume what remains to be proven, namely, that Revelation is an apocalypse.

Similarity to Prophecy

Revelation possesses all the traits of Old Testament prophecy. Revelation looks like prophecy in its claim to divine revelation, its visionary form, its auditory form, its angelic activity, its

---

[9] For a discussion of proposed definitions for *apocalypse* and their disagreement, see Hand, *The Worthy Champion*, 21–39. See also the lengthy treatments in D. S. Russell, *The Method and Message of Jewish Apocalyptic* (Philadelphia: Westminster Press, 1964); H. H. Rowley, *The Relevance of Apocalyptic: A Study of Jewish and Christian Apocalypses from Daniel to the Revelation*, rev. ed. (London: Lutterworth Press, 1963); Bailey, 30–42; and Robert L. Webb, 115–26. These works demonstrate that there is no coherent list of the qualities that make a work apocalyptic. Interpreters must assume what they hope to prove. Even after decades have passed, the situation has not changed. John Bailey wrote in 1905 that "in the enumeration of these various features which are alleged to characterize apocalyptic it must become apparent that no little confusion exists" (36), and eighty-five years later Robert Webb reiterated the same problem.

[10] Leon Morris, *Apocalyptic* (Grand Rapids: Eerdmans, 1972), 20.

description of John's psychological response, its predictions of the future, its discussions of the past, its emphasis on judgment and salvation, its recognition of the centrality of Messiah (Christ), and its ethical demands on its readers. In fact, Ladd observes, "With the exception of Enoch 92–105, there is almost no ethical exhortation in the entire corpus of non-canonical apocalyptic literature," but ethical exhortation occurs repeatedly in Revelation (e.g., Rev. 14:7; 18:4; see also table 15 in chapter 5).[11] This insistent ethical focus makes Revelation far more like the prophetic books of Scripture than like an apocalypse.

In addition Revelation lacks those features that distinguish apocalyptic literature from other literary forms. For example, the apocalypses used pseudonymous authorship and "prophecy" after an event occurred (they pretended to be prophesying a future event by writing of past events under the name of a long-dead figure in Jewish history).[12] Revelation uses neither pseudonymity nor false prophecy. All of the known apocalypses are works of fiction. Revelation expresses reality. All of the apocalypses stem from

---

[11] George Eldon Ladd, "Why Not Prophetic-Apocalyptic?" *Journal of Biblical Literature* 76, no. 3 (September 1957): 192–200. Ladd believes that the term *prophetic-apocalyptic* describes the canonical books better, but the distance between the canonical books and the Jewish apocalypses in tone, content, and origin is so great that it is simpler and more meaningful to recognize the canonical books as simply prophecy. When writers must qualify virtually every characteristic of apocalyptic literature in order to apply it to Revelation, their assessment of Revelation's apocalyptic character loses strength.

[12] These features are so highly characteristic that Bailey claims apocalypses are "almost invariably pseudonymous" (34). He then lists Daniel and Revelation among the Pseudepigrapha. Bailey argues that pseudonymous writing characterized the entire era, however, and sees most of the OT books as pseudonymous as well. John J. Collins (a member of the SBL Genres Project) concurs that "apocalyptic revelations are substantially *ex eventu*, or after the fact." He believes Daniel was written at the end of Onias III's high priesthood (ca. 170 BC), and he rejects the accuracy of Jeremiah's 70 years. "Prophecy and Fulfillment in the Qumran Scrolls," *Journal of the Evangelical Theological Society* 30, no. 3 (September 1987): 271–72. Many conservatives take their theological bearings and their understanding of biblical genres from such men who reject the prophecies of the Old Testament.

human authors and were written on their own human initiative, for their own religiously pragmatic purposes. Revelation derives from a divine Author, on His initiative, and for His purposes.

Some writers believe that apocalypse and prophecy were so closely related that their components intermixed.[13] Although there are some similarities between the two genres, apocalypses arose *because of* "the cessation of prophecy."[14] Either Revelation is prophecy, or it is apocalypse. It cannot be both. Some of the alleged similarities between prophecy and apocalypse appear absurd when evaluated critically. For example, writers classify apocalypse as revelatory literature, but the writers of apocalypses never received a single vision or word from God. No revelation actually occurred.[15] The apocalypse writers made up the symbols, the plots, and the events of their works. In fact, apocalypses *required* the use of rampant symbolism in order to obscure the spiritual emptiness of their works. Classifying Revelation as apocalypse, a post-prophetic, falsely revelatory genre, hardly does justice to its internal claims.

If scientists were trying to compose a definition or classification for "dog," and they included in their group of "dogs" (from which to build their definition) a German shepherd, a Saint Bernard, a

---

[13] See Robert P. Carroll, "Twilight of Prophecy or Dawn of Apocalyptic?" *Journal for the Study of the Old Testament* 14 (1979): 4. Carroll shows how Paul Hanson's *The Dawn of Apocalyptic* blurs the distinction between prophecy and apocalypse.

[14] Morris, *Apocalyptic*, 24. "The writers of this [apocalyptic] class of literature did not usually claim direct inspiration like the prophets. They did not apparently feel themselves as directly moved by God. And in any case, by their time men seem to have been agreed that the prophetic canon had closed" (50). "Prophecy was held in the very highest esteem, but it had ceased" (50). H. H. Rowley also affirms that prophecy and apocalypse are distinct. A work of literature could not be both (91).

[15] Bailey believes that sheer imagination lies behind all of the apocalypses. He traces other proposed origins, including Persian mythology and Hellenization, and finds them deficient explanations. "The only source upon which they could draw was their imagination, and to it they gave free reign" (40).

poodle, a Labrador retriever, a pug, and a Siamese cat, they would run into a significant problem. Once they included the cat in the category of *dog*, their definition could not turn out well. They would either have to over-generalize their definition with the result that it would have diminished value in distinguishing actual dogs, or they could define true "dogness" based on the majority of the animals in the group and force the cat into the category unnaturally. This is what we have with the definition of *apocalypse*. Including Daniel, Ezekiel, Zechariah, and Revelation in the category of apocalypse produces an over-generalized definition or forces the biblical books into a category that they do not really fit. They are works of prophecy. They are not apocalypses. Their category-distinctiveness lies in their deriving from God rather than from the imagination of men.[16]

Logical Circularity

Since Revelation possesses elements that distinguish it from the apocalyptic books and lacks elements that would ally it with those books, most of the arguments in favor of Revelation-as-apocalypse amount to circular reasoning. They claim that Revelation is an apocalypse because it is highly symbolic, then they deduce its symbolism from the "fact" that it is an apocalypse.[17]

---

[16] The dog-cat illustration works so well since dogs and cats share so many common traits. They eat the same types of foods and have the same basic body plan (at least to the ordinary, non-technical observer). So are dogs merely social cats, or are cats merely fastidious, egocentric, loner dogs? Neither. Their classification stems ultimately from God's design of them (their origin).

[17] Emil Schürer considers esoteric symbolism to be one of the distinguishing features of apocalypses. He also observes that the symbols used in the apocalypses are so complex and undefined that the interpreter must guess at the meaning. *A History of the Jewish People in the Time of Christ*, vol. 2 (Edinburgh: T. & T. Clark, 1886), 46. If Schürer is correct, and Revelation is an apocalypse, then the value of Revelation for God's people diminishes accordingly.

Anachronism and Misunderstanding of Terms

The tired assumption that since Revelation begins with the phrase "the apocalypse of Jesus Christ" it must be apocalyptic literature provides a classic example of both anachronism and poor exegesis.[18] Interpreters who ought to know better often argue this point as evidence that Revelation is an apocalypse. As far as careful grammatical-historical investigation has found, the Greek term *apocalypse* (ἀποκάλυψις) meant simply "revelation," "disclosure," or "unveiling." It did not denote a genre until the early nineteenth century. A brief examination of the introductions to the extant Jewish apocalypses that predate the New Testament in table 17 illustrates this fact. Extant apocalypses rarely begin in the same fashion as Revelation begins, and they do not use the designation *apocalypse* as an indication of their genre.[19]

[18] Alan Bandy commits this anachronistic error in "The Hermeneutics of Symbolism: How to Interpret the Symbols of John's Apocalypse," *Southern Baptist Journal of Theology* 14, no. 1 (Spring 2010): 48.

[19] One exception lies in 3 Baruch, whose Greek text reads, Διήγησις καὶ ἀποκάλυψις Βαροὺχ περὶ ὧν κελεύματι θεοῦ ἀρρήτων εἶδεν. Εὐλόγησον δέσποτα. ᾿Αποκαλυψις Βαροὺχ, ὃς ἔστιν ἐπὶ ποταμοῦ Γέλ., κλαίων ὑπὲρ τῆς αἰχμαλωσίας Ἱερουσαλήμ. Three problems attend this work. First, the book was written between AD 130 and the third century AD and thus postdates Revelation and cannot effectively comment on the genre of its antecedent. Second, both a translator and a later redactor worked over the Hebrew/Aramaic original at some point, leaving the original text in question. Third, it remains unclear whether the author intended a genre designation by the word *apocalypse*. Thus, the evidence (1) postdates Revelation and (2) remains highly ambiguous. The writings of some church fathers refer to additional Gnostic "apocalypses," but since we possess no extant manuscripts of these writings, we cannot analyze them concerning their introductory claims. Thus, George Eldon Ladd is essentially correct when he observes that the term *apokalypsis* "is found in the apocalyptic literature only in the NT Apocalypse" ("Why Not Prophetic-Apocalyptic?" 192). Alexander Kulik observes, "The use of any equivalent term as a title or genre definition is not attested in the present corpus of Hebrew or Aramaic texts." *3 Baruch: Greek-Slavonic Apocalypse of Baruch* (Berlin: Walter de Gruyter, 2010), 92.

Table 17—A Comparison of Book Introductions[20]

Document	Introduction
Revelation	**The Revelation of Jesus Christ, which God gave unto him, to shew unto his servants things which must shortly come to pass; and he sent and signified it by his angel unto his servant John.**
Jubilees	This is the history of the division of the days of the law and of the testimony, of the events of the years, of their (year) weeks, of their Jubilees throughout all the years of the world, as the Lord spake to Moses on Mount Sinai
The Life of Adam and Eve	When they were driven out from paradise, they made themselves a booth, and spent seven days mourning and lamenting in great grief.
1 Enoch	The words of the blessing of Enoch, wherewith he blessed the elect and righteous, who will be living in the day of tribulation, when all the wicked and godless are to be removed. And he took up his parable and said . . .
The Testaments of the Twelve Patriarchs	The copy of the Testament of Reuben, even the commands which he gave his sons before he died in the hundred and twenty-fifth year of his life . . .
The Sibylline Oracles, Book III	O thou who thunderest from on high, blessed heavenly one, who has the Cherubim as thy throne, I pray thee give me a short respite from mine unerring oracle for my soul within me is weary.
The Assumption of Moses	The testament of Moses even the things which he commanded in the one hundred and twentieth year of his life, that is the two thousand five hundredth year from the creation of the world.
2 Enoch	There was a wise man, a great artificer, and the Lord conceived love for him and received him, that he should behold the uppermost dwellings and be an eye-witness of the wise and great and inconceivable and immutable realm of God Almighty, of the very wonderful and glorious and bright and many-eyed station of the Lord's servants, and of the inaccessible throne of the Lord.
3 Baruch	A narrative and revelation of Baruch, concerning those ineffable things which he saw by the command of God. Bless Thou, O Lord. A revelation of Baruch who stood upon the river Gel weeping over the captivity of Jerusalem.
4 Ezra	In the thirtieth year after the downfall of the city I—Salathiel (who am also Ezra)—was in Babylon, and as I lay upon my bed I was disquieted [gap in the MSS] and my mind was preoccupied with my thoughts because I saw Sion's desolation on the one hand (matched) with the abundant wealth of Babylon's inhabitants on the other.

[20] All of the apocalyptic works cited in the table appear in R. H. Charles, *Pseudepigrapha*, vol. 2 of *The Apocrypha and Pseudepigrapha of the Old Testament in English* (1914; repr., Oxford: Oxford University Press, 1963).

Document	Introduction
The Apocalypse of Abraham[21]	The Book of the Apocalypse of Abraham, son of Terah, son of Nahor, son of Serug . . .

Explicit Internal Claims

Revelation claims to be a work of prophecy and gives crucial internal evidence to warrant that claim.[22] First, in 1:3; 19:10; 22:7, 10, 18, and 19, Revelation uses the term *prophecy* to describe the content and genre of the book. In addition an angel refers to John as among the prophets (22:9), John receives instruction to "prophesy again" (10:11), and Revelation is called the testimony of Jesus (1:2, 9).[23] Since *prophēteia* (προφητεία) already existed as a term that carried theological and literary weight even as an accepted genre designation, and *apokalypsis* (ἀποκάλυψις) did not, John's use of *prophēteia* makes a truth claim and a genre claim that the interpreter ought not lightly dismiss.

Second, the expression "these things saith . . ." (*tade legei*; τάδε λέγει) appears in the introduction to each of the seven churches. These Greek words reflect an archaic and unmistakably prophetic formula. Outside of Revelation they occur only once in the New Testament (Acts 21:11). In that passage Agabus prophesies,

---

[21] Kulik's claim that several other Greek works use *apocalypsis* as a genre designation is not entirely convincing. For example, he lists the Apocalypse of Abraham (which is extant only in Slavonic), the Testament of Abraham (where *apocalypse* occurs only in a later recension), and Gnostic and late Christian apocalypses (whose dates cannot determine John's use of the term since they post-date Revelation). Kulik, 92.

[22] "While the precise differentiation of prophecy from apocalyptic is not easy, it can scarcely be denied that a broad distinction may be made between the two. No one, surely, will contend that prophecy and apocalyptic are synonymous terms. It is then significant that our author specifically classes his book with the prophets. In line with this is the fact that his visions convey the word of God" (Morris, *Apocalyptic*, 78).

[23] "It is from the prophetic circles in this group of Churches that the one great literary product of early Christian prophecy emanates. . . . Both in the prologue and epilogue, the work of John lays claim to a prophetic character" (Swete, *The Apocalypse of St John*, xvi).

"Thus saith the Holy Ghost." In the Septuagint, by the time of the prophetic books, they occur most commonly (almost exclusively) in the expression "Thus saith the Lord." John's use of an archaic expression that has indisputable connections with Old Testament prophecy supports the claim that his book possesses the same quality. Table 18 illustrates the prophetic usage of this word. Significantly, Revelation casts Jesus Christ in the place of God. The Old Testament said, "Thus saith the Lord." Revelation says, "Thus saith . . ." and then uses titles and descriptions of Christ. Jesus is the Lord.

TABLE 18—Τάδε λέγει IN THE PROPHETS AND THE NEW TESTAMENT

Description	Number	Example
Total OT occurrences of τάδε λέγει In non-prophetic books In prophetic books	243 verses 79 verses 164 verses	Isaiah 1:24, "Therefore saith the Lord, the Lord of hosts, the mighty One of Israel . . ."
Total OT occurrences lacking God as speaker In non-prophetic books In prophetic books	21 verses 16 verses 5 verses[24]	Amos 7:11, "For thus Amos saith, Jeroboam shall die by the sword . . . ."
Total NT occurrences of τάδε λέγει Outside Revelation	8 verses 1 verse	Acts 21:11, "Thus saith the Holy Ghost, So shall the Jews at Jerusalem bind the man that owneth this girdle, . . ."
Total having God as the divine Revealer	222 verses	

The failure to admit the prophetic quality of Revelation obscures some of its profound theological statements concerning Christ's

[24] Four of these five occurrences in the prophetic books that lack God as the speaker simply repeat the history from 2 Kings 18–19 concerning Rabshakeh and Hezekiah's interaction. The final one, used here as an example (Amos 7:11), has the wicked Amaziah lying about Amos by claiming that Amos is the source of his (so-called) prophecy. Amos protests that God was the source. Thus the case for the consistent usage of "Thus saith" becomes even stronger.

deity and offices. Rejecting the prophetic genre has Christological repercussions since it places the words of Christ outside His prophetic office. To what would that reduce Him? An apocalyptic visionary? A post-prophetic pseudo-seer? In this case, the clarity and weight of Christ's words would fall short of the clarity and weight of the merely human prophets of the Old Testament. His words alone, among all the prophetic words of the Old and New Testaments, would contribute nothing to doctrine and nothing to our understanding of the present age or the age to come. We already know from the other canonical books that Christ watches over His people, that God reigns in heaven, that believers suffer persecution from this world, that Satan opposes the church, that Christ will return again to judge the world, and that He will reign in eternity. Taking Revelation as an apocalypse reduces the book to this content, eviscerating its contributions both to theology in general and to eschatology in particular.

Third, Revelation alludes to Old Testament prophecy more frequently than any other book of the Bible. Commentators typically estimate that between 250 and 700 distinct Old Testament allusions appear in Revelation.[25] John writes self-consciously in the line of the prophets.[26] Table 19 below represents this phenomenon by citing the allusions to Isaiah that appear in Revelation. Revelation makes similarly numerous allusions to Psalms, Jeremiah, Ezekiel, Daniel, and Zechariah. Couch estimates that Revelation alludes to at least twenty-four of the thirty-nine Old Testament books.[27] Since

[25] The following figures represent the estimated OT allusions in Revelation by specific commentators: R. H. Charles (250); H. B. Swete (278); M. Tenney and M. Couch (348); Marty (453); Gelin (518); UBS Greek New Testament (634); Staehelin (700).

[26] See for example, R. H. Charles, *Revelation of St John,* 1:lxvii–lxxxii.

[27] "Using the Greek Septuagint, John alluded to each of the five books of Moses, Joshua, Judges, 2 Samuel, 2 Kings, 1 Chronicles, Nehemiah, Psalms, Proverbs, the major prophetic books, and seven of the minor prophets—twenty-four books in all."

Revelation draws so heavily on the Old Testament, one cannot spiritualize it without doing violence to the expectations of Old Testament prophecy. This observation demonstrates that there are consequences to the mishandling of Revelation. Interpreting Revelation symbolically yields a symbolic interpretation of prophecy throughout the canon.

TABLE 19—ALLUSIONS TO ISAIAH IN REVELATION

ISAIAH		REVELATION	
enter into the rock and hide . . . for fear of the Lord . . . and [enter] into the caves	2:10, 19	they hid themselves in the dens and in the rocks of the mountains . . . from the face of him that sitteth	6:15–16
each one had six wings	6:2	each of them [having] six wings above	4:8
said, Holy, holy, holy, is the Lord of hosts	6:3	saying, Holy, holy, holy, Lord God Almighty	4:8
the house was filled with smoke	6:4	the temple was filled with smoke from the glory of God	15:8
the morning star fell from heaven	14:12	there fell a great star from heaven	8:10
to . . . the work of his hands	17:8	of the works of their hands	9:20
Babylon is fallen, is fallen	21:9	Babylon is fallen, is fallen	14:8
And the key of the house of David will I lay upon his shoulder; so he shall open, and none shall shut; and he shall shut, and none shall open.	22:22	he that hath the key of David, he that openeth, and no man shutteth; and shutteth, and no man openeth	3:7
whose merchants are princes, whose traffickers are the honourable of the earth	23:8	thy merchants were the great men of the earth	18:23
and the Lord God will wipe away tears from off all faces	25:8	and God shall wipe away all tears from their eyes	7:17
the heavens shall be rolled together as a scroll all [the stars] shall fall . . . as a falling fig from the fig tree.	34:4	the stars . . . fell unto the earth, even as a fig tree casteth her untimely figs And the heaven departed as a scroll when it is rolled together	6:13 6:14

Mal Couch, ed., *A Bible Handbook to Revelation* (Grand Rapids: Kregel Publications, 2001), 71.

ISAIAH		REVELATION	
It shall not be quenched night nor day; the smoke thereof shall go up for ever	34:10	the smoke of their torment ascendeth up for ever and ever	14:11
his reward is with him	40:10	my reward is with me	22:12
I have loved thee	43:4	I have loved thee	3:9
Behold, I will do a new thing	43:19	behold I make all things new	21:5
I am the first and I am the last I am the first, I also am the last	44:6; 48:12	I am the first and the last	1:17; 2:8; 22:13
[they] shall come over unto thee . . . [and] fall down unto thee	45:14	I will make them to come and worship before thy feet	3:9
thou saidst, I shall be a lady for ever: . . . that sayest in thine heart, . . . I shall not sit as a widow"	47:7–8	she saith in her heart, I sit a queen, and am no widow	18:7
I have shewed thee new things from this time	48:6	[I show to you] things which shall be hereafter	1:19
he hath made my mouth like a sharp sword	49:2	out of his mouth went a sharp two-edged sword	1:16
They shall not hunger nor thirst; neither shall the heat nor sun smite them: for [God] shall lead them, even by the springs of water shall he guide them.	49:10	They shall hunger no more, neither thirst any more; neither shall the sun light on them, nor any heat. For the Lamb . . . shall feed them, and shall lead them unto living fountains of waters	7:16–17
which hast drunk at the hand of the Lord the cup of his fury	51:17	he shall drink of the wine of the wrath of God	14:10
Jerusalem, the holy city . . . there shall no more come into thee . . . the unclean	52:1	there shall in no wise enter into it any thing that defileth	21:27
neither [is] deceit in his mouth	53:9	in their mouth was found no guile	14:5
I will lay . . . thy foundations with sapphire . . . and all thy borders of pleasant stones	54:11–12	the building of the wall of it was of jasper . . . the second [foundation], sapphire	21:18–19
every one that thirsteth, come ye to the waters . . . [without] money	55:1	I will give unto him that is athirst . . . freely	21:6

ISAIAH		REVELATION	
Gentiles shall come to thy light, and kings to the brightness of thy rising	60:3	the nations of them which are saved shall walk in the light of it: and the kings of the earth do bring their glory and honour into it	21:24
thy gates shall be open continually; they shall not be shut day nor night	60:11	the gates of it shall not be shut at all by day: for there shall be no night there	21:25
The sun shall be no more thy light by day; . . . but the Lord shall be unto thee an everlasting light	60:19	the city had no need of the sun, neither of the moon, . . . for the glory of God did lighten it	21:23
he hath clothed me . . . as a bride adorneth herself with jewels	61:10	as a bride adorned for her husband	21:2
thou shalt be called by a new name	62:2	a new name	2:17; 3:12
I will tread down the people in mine anger	63:6	cast it into the great winepress of the wrath of God. And the winepress was trodden	14:19
I create new heavens and a new earth	65:17 (66:22)	a new heaven and a new earth	21:1

Fourth, Revelation's introductory formula matches Old Testament prophetic introductory formulas. The Old Testament prophetic books follow two patterns. In the first pattern the name of the prophet follows a revelatory term. In the second pattern the elements of divine impetus (the Lord is giving the revelation) and motion carry over to the prophet. Table 20 demonstrates this phenomenon. Revelation actually follows both patterns by casting Jesus Christ in the primary role of the prophet and John in a secondary prophetic role. Revelation imitates Old Testament prophetic formulas, strengthening the case that it, too, is a work of prophecy.

TABLE 20—PROPHETIC INTRODUCTORY FORMULAS

Reference	Revelatory Term	Prophet
Isaiah 1:1	the vision	of Isaiah
Jeremiah 1:1	the words	of Jeremiah

Reference	Revelatory Term	Prophet
Amos 1:1	the words	of Amos
Obadiah 1:1	the vision	of Obadiah
Nahum 1:1	the book of the vision	of Nahum
Habakkuk 1:1	the oracle	which Habakkuk saw
Malachi 1:1	the oracle of the word of the Lord to Israel	through Malachi

Reference	Revelatory Term, Divine Impetus, Motion	Prophet Recipient
Ezekiel 1:3	the word of the Lord came expressly	unto Ezekiel
Hosea 1:1	the word of the Lord that came	unto Hosea
Joel 1:1	the word of the Lord that came	to Joel
Jonah 1:1	the word of the Lord came	unto Jonah
Micah 1:1	the word of the Lord that came	to Micah
Zephaniah 1:1	the word of the Lord which came	unto Zephaniah
Haggai 1:1	came the word of the Lord	by Haggai
Zechariah 1:1	came the word of the Lord	unto Zechariah
Revelation 1:1	**the revelation**	**of Jesus Christ**
	he sent	**to John**

Undermining Biblical Integrity

To be consistent, conservative writers who accept Revelation as an apocalypse should assert the same genre for Daniel, Ezekiel, Zechariah, and parts of Joel, Isaiah, and Zephaniah. This assertion would seem to indicate that all of these books were fraudulent since apocalypses did not exist until 200 BC, a time well after the books claim to have been written. Liberals have no problem with this assessment, but conservatives resist this logical conclusion by positing one of two rebuttals. We can expand the dates of apocalyptic literature to 600 BC–AD 150, but this expanded dating flies in the face of all the non-canonical evidence. This is the expedient chosen by most conservative writers. Alternately, we can reject the critical assessment of these Old Testament books as apocalypses. Once we do so, we cannot escape the fact that Revelation's conscious connection lies with the Old Testament and not with the popular culture of its day. This requires that we reassess Revelation's genre as prophetic.

Relevance of Truth Claims

Finally, since apocalypses were, in essence, visionary false predictions concerning the future, they were as close to real prophecy as the *Chronicles of Narnia* are to a biography of C. S. Lewis. Mistaking the genre of Revelation sets the interpreter up for hermeneutical failure. By applying the wrong rules to the interpretation of a text, the reader comes to wrong conclusions. For example, some devoted readers of Sherlock Holmes, failing to recognize Doyle's writings as fiction, actually believe Holmes exists. He receives many letters each year requesting his help. But he is imaginary! In the reverse of this situation, interpreters assign Revelation (non-fiction) to the category of apocalypse (fiction). The genre *apocalypse* is fiction.[28] This conclusion cannot be avoided. It makes pseudo-prophetic claims, has no basis in reality, and reflects entirely the imagination of the author(s). Apocalyptic literature contradicts the Scriptures rather than confirming them.[29] Revelation hardly fits this category.[30] Taking Revelation as an apocalypse undermines its truth claims.

---

[28] The liberal James Hardy Ropes uses the "fact" that Revelation is an apocalypse to reduce the book to "a worthy expression of the human spirit" since, once a book is taken as an apocalypse, it is a product of the writer's own imagination and does not have divine authority. "The Reasonable Appeal of the Book of Revelation," *Harvard Theological Review* 12, no. 4 (October 1919): 426.

[29] For example, 4 Ezra proclaims that the Messiah will come at the end of time, reign for four hundred years, and die along with all of His followers (6.35–9.25). Third Baruch makes Michael the mediator between saints and God. Michael will reward people based on their good works.

[30] In addition, the social conditions that lie behind apocalyptic literature and Revelation differ. "The socio-religious movement that produced the Apocalypse [the book of Revelation] is the one begun by Jesus and continued by the apostles, not the apocalyptic spirit that developed among the Jews following the abuses of Antiochus

Conclusion to the Genre Argument

Apocalypses communicate through opaque symbolism. While they convey a general message through specific images, they often lack recognizable connections with specific times, places, and events. They are, like the Delphic Oracle, false prophecies, open generalities, mystic impressions, wild fantasies, and imaginative visions. The similarities between Revelation and Old Testament prophecy argue strongly that Revelation is simply prophetic. This fact does not prove that Revelation is literal, but it strongly implies that fact. Prophecy could be symbolic, at least theoretically, but it has not tended to be. However, once we recognize Revelation as prophetic, we cut the necessary connection between it and symbolic interpretation. We return to ordinary, consistent, probable exegesis as it applies to the rest of Scripture. If Revelation is prophetic, its genre cannot serve as the warrant for a symbolic method.

The Interpretation of *Signified* (1:1)

A recent argument for the symbolic method relies on the meaning of the word *signified* in Revelation 1:1.[31] This argument asserts that (1) since this word relates to the noun *sign* (σημεῖον), (2) since it appears in Daniel 2:30 and 2:45 in a context of symbolic imagery, and (3) since it can mean "to signify" or "to show by a sign," this

---

Epiphanes" (Thomas, *Revelation 1–7*, 24). The purposes of prophecy and apocalypse differ. The former rests more frequently on the centrality of God and His work; the latter focuses on the plight of the community.

[31] G. K. Beale supports this argument in his commentary on Revelation (50–55). He calls it a "clear allusion" to Dan. 2:28–30, 45 and builds upon the pictorial images in Daniel's vision to require a symbolic interpretation of the entire book of Revelation (50). He defuses some criticism by admitting that the common meaning of *signify* (σημαίνω) is simply "to make known," "indicate," or "declare," but he wrongly assumes that he has proven his case. All that he has actually achieved is to show that the word *signify* appears in a context in Daniel where symbols also occur. No one denies this fact. He has not established that "signify" *means* "to speak in symbols." Alan Bandy accepts Beale's assertion rather uncritically in "The Hermeneutics of Symbolism," 48.

word warrants the application of the symbolic method of interpretation to the entire book of Revelation.

Several exegetical considerations help us assess the validity of the argument based on the meaning of *signified.* First, defining a word based on its cognates (or word roots) is a hazardous linguistic procedure. No one can deny that *sēmainō* (Rev. 1:1) relates to a cognate noun *sēmeion*, but claiming that they possess the same meaning oversteps the evidence. Studies of grammar and vocabulary indicate that cognates often branch off and assume meanings independently of each other. The words *shirt* and *skirt* provide a good example. Although they both derive from the same Old English word (*scyrte*), they have substantially different meanings today. Making one mean the other exhibits a linguistic fallacy.[32] Likewise, although the Greek noun and verb forms built on the *sēm-* stem are related, they do not communicate the same idea.[33]

Second, the appearance of an ordinary word within the context of some symbolic imagery does not turn the common sense of that word into a symbolic sense. This assumption violates the rules of language. It also makes symbols unintelligible since there would be no way to explain a symbol with ordinary language. Every attempt to do so would convert the ordinary words into symbols themselves. The *image* that Nebuchadnezzar saw in his dream was a

---

[32] See D. A. Carson's *Exegetical Fallacies*, 2nd ed. (Grand Rapids: Baker Books, 1996), 28–33, for an explanation of the root fallacy.

[33] Some figurative interpreters press this misuse of cognates to new levels. William E. Cox argues backward from the English translation "to signify" in saying, "This word means just what the syllables say: sign-i-fied. The Greek word 'signify' means to speak in sign language, to make use of symbols, numerology, figures of speech, and so forth" (65). Besides the linguistic fallacy of reading the etymology of a translation back into an original language, this argument makes up its own definition based on Greek cognates. This is not legitimate word study. Had Cox done even rudimentary analysis of the use of this word in Scripture, he could not have offered a definition so far off the mark. Table 21 illustrates this conclusion.

symbol. The text clearly expresses this fact. But the context has the capacity to communicate the meaning of the vision only because the remaining words in the text remain non-symbolic. They are straightforwardly literal. Literal interpretation allows for the existence of symbols without making the entire text symbolic. With reference to Daniel 2:30 and 2:45, the symbolic method has not established adequate warrant for abandoning the common understanding of the meaning of the Greek word "to make known."

Third, *sēmainō* most frequently means "to declare," "to indicate," or "to make known." It appears thirty-one times in the Bible and Apocrypha, but most of these instances have no connection with symbolism. Table 21 illustrates the Old Testament use of the term. The case becomes even more favorable toward a literal interpretation when we recognize that the only occurrences that might help the case for symbolic interpretation are the very passages in question. In the two of these passages that Beale uses to establish his case (Dan. 2:30 and 2:45), the context strongly favors the meaning "to make known." God is "indicating" to Nebuchadnezzar what the future holds. The fact that God chose a visionary "indication" in this particular instance does not make "indication" always visionary. While it is true that Nebuchadnezzar had a dream and that his dream was symbolic, the context requires a normal meaning for the verb "to make known." In addition, the Hebrew word in Daniel is the ordinary Aramaic word for "making known" (*yeda'*). It has no connotation of symbolic reference at all. The interpreter who claims that *sēmainō* in Revelation 1:1 proves the symbolic method is engaging in wishful thinking.

The New Testament's use of *sēmainō* corroborates the Old Testament usage. In Acts 25:27 *sēmainō must* mean "to specify or to make known," because the Roman legal system required clear notice of the charges against a Roman citizen. This requirement is precisely what troubled Festus. He had to send Paul to Rome, but he could not provide any legal basis for Paul's imprisonment. Furthermore, in John 12:33 and 18:32 the word must also mean "to indicate" since Christ spoke literally of His being "lifted up" on a cross and the necessity of a Roman, not a Jewish, execution.

Table 21—The Use of "Signify" in the Scriptures and Apocrypha

Meaning	References
To make known, declare, indicate	Exod. 18:20; 1 Esd. 2:2; 8:48; Esther 2:22; 2 Macc. 2:1; 11:17; Dan. 2:15; 2:23; John 12:33; 18:32; 21:19; Acts 11:28; 25:27
To make noise, blow upon, or announce (with a trumpet)	Num. 10:9; Josh. 6:8; 2 Chron. 13:12; Neh. 8:15; Job 39:24, 25; Jer. 4:5; 6:1; Ezek. 33:3, 6
To cry out, shout, call out	Judg. 7:21; Ezra 3:11; Zech. 10:8
To signal (may relate to *indicate* above)	Prov. 6:13
Meaning in dispute or under discussion	Dan. 2:30; 2:45; Rev. 1:1

The Problem of Comprehensibility

The symbolic method assumes that the audience in a given age—whether the sixth century BC or first century AD—would understand the symbols in a document. The evidence that we have from the few known symbols in Scripture implies exactly the opposite. When Ezekiel, Daniel, Zechariah, and John received symbolic communication, they had no idea what it meant. There was no preexisting "key" to unlock these revelatory symbols. The prophets themselves remained ignorant until an angel interpreted the figures for them.[34] If the known symbols were incoherent to

[34] "There are many revelational dreams in the Scripture which utilize figures and symbols unfamiliar to the prophets. These 'signs' of the future come to the prophets devoid of what is contemporary, instinctive, and familiar. In Daniel 7, the prophet sees four beasts which appear so unfamiliar and unearthly that he has to use analogies (e.g. 'like a lion'). But the fourth beast is so unlike anything Daniel has ever seen that he does not bother to use an earthly analogy in reporting to his readers" (Tan, 84).

the prophets without interpretation, how could an entirely symbolic book have been coherent for a first-century Gentile church (or for any church)? The assumption of a symbolic interpretation of Revelation removes the possibility of its proper exegesis from the purview of the church.[35] An assumption more consistent with both the truth claims of Revelation and the nature of the remainder of Scripture is that while Revelation clearly uses symbols at some points, its interpretation is predominantly literal.

The New Testament's Spiritual Application of the Old

If theologians could demonstrate that the New Testament regularly spiritualizes the Old Testament covenants and prophecies, they would substantially weaken the case for a literal interpretation of prophecy.

The Case for the New Testament's Spiritual Application of the Old

The claim that the New Testament spiritualizes the covenants and prophecies of the Old Testament rests on two primary claims. First, Israel forfeited the reception of its national promises because of its final, formal rejection of the Messiah.[36] Second, the church

[35]Even as eminent a theologian as Warfield could succumb to this weak and entirely subjective view of the book. See Benjamin Breckinridge Warfield, *Biblical Doctrines* (Oxford, 1932; repr., Grand Rapids: Baker Book House, 2003), 650, in which the author says, "We must bear in mind that the book we are reading is written in symbols and gives us a direct description of nothing that it sets before us, but always a direct description only of the symbol by which it is represented," and, "we are not to expect a direct description of the 'intermediate state': were such a description given, that would be evidence enough that the intermediate state was not intended, but was rather the symbol of something else." Reasoning such as this refutes itself as an absurd principle of interpretation and language. In simple terms Warfield claims the following: we know that if anything in Revelation seems to mean anything, then it cannot mean that thing, because nothing means what it appears to mean. He provides an extreme example of the subjectivity inherent in a symbolic method of interpretation.

[36] Symbolic interpreters vary about the extent to which racial Jews will turn to Christ in the future. Most argue that although Israel has spiritual existence identical with the

is the new, spiritual Israel, and as such it inherits the covenants, promises, and prophecies in spiritualized, idealized form.

Preterists believe that Israel's rejection of Christ led directly to the destruction of Jerusalem in AD 70. Historicists, idealists, and amillennialists assert that Israel's crucifying Christ led to an immediate and irretrievable loss of all material promises of the Abrahamic and Davidic covenants. Some writers assert that while the material promises ceased to exist, the spiritual promises continued to be in force. They try to marshal support from several passages (Gen. 12:3; 22:18; Rom. 2:28–29; 4:17; Eph. 2:11–16; 3:6–9; Phil. 3:3; Col. 2:11).[37] However, thousands of Jews believed in their Messiah (Acts 2:42), and even many priests came to faith (Acts 6:7). There was no final, formal rejection of Messiah by the Jews, though their leaders did reject Him in a fashion that led to divine retribution in the destruction of Jerusalem.

Direct scriptural statements backing the claim that the church is the new spiritual Israel are extremely limited, but inferences and principles abound.[38] A similarity seems to exist between the

---

church, and while racial Jews can share in this spiritual existence, Israel has no separate, national existence in God's plan following the destruction of Jerusalem.

[37] This series of references comes from William E. Cox's argument for symbolic interpretation in *Amillennialism Today*, 37. In other words, these are the best warrant that spiritual interpreters can find for their position.

[38] For example, even in a book purporting to address the interrelationship of Israel and the Church, Oswald T. Allis sets out only twenty-one passages that he claims apply prophecies to the church that were originally given to Israel. None of his examples provide adequate warrant for his claim. His supporting passages fall into several categories: (1) An OT passage *not directly connected with Israel* has literal fulfillment not in the church but in events surrounding the creation of the church (Acts 1:20); (2) the NT writers merely allude to an OT prophetic passage as an illustration, not as a fulfillment (Rom. 9:25–26); (3) a fulfillment of a general OT prophecy tries to force the church to exist in the OT (anachronistic fallacy) (Acts 2:16–40); (4) the NT passage has only the vaguest, most tenuous connection with the OT but is cited anyway (Acts 1:8); and (5) simple misrepresentation of what the NT passage actually says (1 Pet. 1:10–12). *Prophecy*

Hebrew *congregation* and the New Testament *assembly* (church). Jewish and Gentile believers clearly have some connection since Christ has broken down the middle wall separating the two (Eph. 2:14–16). And Galatians 6:16 can be construed as supporting the position if one selects an unlikely interpretation of the word *and.*

Assessment of the Case for the New Testament's Spiritual Application of the Old

In order to analyze the case for the New Testament's spiritualization of the Old Testament we must examine biblical covenants very carefully. Theologians often impose their modern systems onto the biblical covenants and mar the proper understanding of these covenants by their presuppositions.

The Nature of Biblical Covenants

Two types of covenants exist: bilateral and unilateral. In a bilateral covenant, both parties commit to the covenant, and one party must fulfill his obligations before the other party must fulfill his. A sequence and an implied condition exist. If the first party fails in his obligations, the second party need not fulfill his. Some writers describe such a covenant as *conditional.* In a unilateral covenant, a single party (A) binds himself to another (B). The second party has no responsibility to fulfill any terms. Since only one party secures the covenant, some writers call such a covenant *unconditional.*[39] Figurative interpreters usually assess the Old Testament covenants

---

and the Church (Philadelphia: Presbyterian and Reformed Publishing Company, 1964), 134–59.

[39] Bruce K. Waltke presents an unconvincing and poorly argued case for conditionality in unilateral covenants in "The Phenomenon of Conditionality within Unconditional Covenants," in *Israel's Apostasy and Restoration: Essays in Honor of Roland K. Harrison,* ed. Avraham Gileadi (Grand Rapids: Baker Book House, 1988), 123–39. The reader will sense that he is straining to impose conditions where none occur in the text. For example, he resorts to calling events prior to the formation of the covenant a condition of the covenant.

as bilateral or conditional covenants. They argue that since Israel has failed to meet its obligations, the covenant no longer applies to Israel; therefore, we should expect no millennial kingdom and no material interpretation of prophecy.

If a friend needed his house painted, he could hire me in a business contract that amounts to a bilateral covenant: "If you paint my house within the next two weeks, I will pay you $2,000." In one sense the covenant is conditional since my friend does not need to pay me unless and until I paint his house. Moreover, if I fail to paint his house within the allotted time and he hires another painter to do the job, I cannot expect him to pay me the $2,000 originally agreed upon.

On the other hand, parents often give promises to their children without preconditions. If I promise my children that we will go camping at the end of the summer, I am committing myself to an action without qualifications. I made a unilateral promise. One of the questions that we face in Scripture is this: are the individual biblical covenants bilateral or unilateral? If they are bilateral, then there is at least the potential for failure of the covenant. If they are unilateral (promises), then there is no possibility of failure since God secures the covenant by His own power.

Problems with a Symbolic View of Biblical Covenants

Once we assume that a covenant is bilateral or conditional, we should recognize that a violation of that covenant (a failure of the first party to fulfill its obligations) annuls the covenant entirely. Failure in the part of the first party does not shift the covenant to a new party and new terms. A breach of covenant voids the covenant.[40] On the other hand a unilateral or unconditional covenant requires exact fulfillment of all particulars in the terms it was given.[41] In this case, failure on the part of the covenanter to fulfill his obligations amounts to a breach of his promise (Gal. 3:15–17).[42] No one has a right to add to or change a covenant once the parties have ratified it, and Paul includes God in this equation as One Who has made and ratified His covenant with Abraham. God never subjugated the Abrahamic Covenant to the Mosaic Covenant. He never altered the provisions of the Abrahamic Covenant to reference a *merely* spiritual seed. The physical seed of Abraham must receive the land promise, while the spiritual seed of Abraham must receive the spiritual blessings of the covenant. Figure 4 illustrates this visually.

---

[40] The church can replace Israel in the covenant promises only if the church is an *original* party to the covenant. The Old Testament lists blessings for the Gentiles as *provisions* of the covenant, but the Gentiles were not *parties* to the covenant. This confusion of covenantal *parties* and *provisions* abounds in spiritual interpretation.

[41] John F. Walvoord observes, "The Book of Genesis itself gives constant confirmation that God promised a literal possession of the land by Abraham's posterity, and that Abraham understood it that way." "The Doctrine of Grace in the Interpretation of Prophecy," *Bibliotheca Sacra* 140, no. 558 (1983): 101. The symbolic interpretation of prophecy has a massive burden of proof if it would spiritualize the Old Testament covenants.

[42] Interpreters who deny this biblically warranted assertion appeal to Jeremiah 18:7–10 as if it implies that any and all statements made by God at any and all points of time are conditional and reversible. This is not what Jeremiah 18 is indicating. In fact, internal to the book of Jeremiah are the verses 7:16; 11:14; and 14:11–12, in which God specifically commands Jeremiah *not* to pray for the people since their national judgment is irreversible. (See also 2 Kings 23:25–27, where Josiah's righteousness merely delayed but could not revoke impending judgment.) Jeremiah 18 applies in those general circumstances where God has not unilaterally entered into a covenant (such as the Abrahamic, Davidic, and New covenants). Jeremiah 18 addresses cases such as Jonah's preaching concerning Nineveh's soon demise, where God relents when the people repent, but Jonah's preaching did not involve any type of covenant promise.

FIGURE 4—DISPLAY OF BILATERAL & UNILATERAL COVENANTS

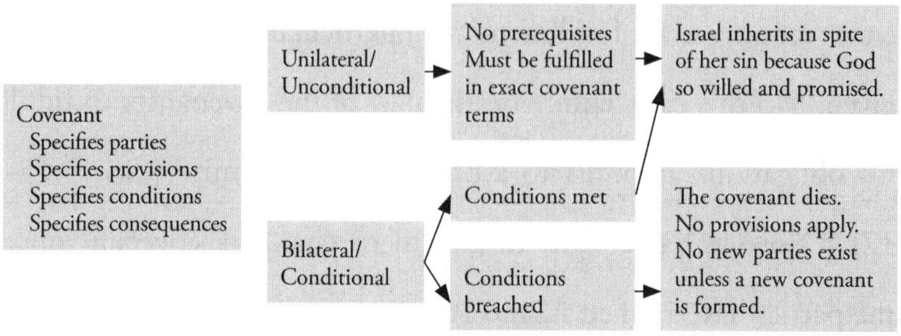

Spiritual interpretations rely on a covenantal impossibility: the granting of a bilateral covenant in shifted terms to a different party once it was breached by one of the original parties. Of course a party to the original covenant (God) can make whatever new covenants He wishes with new parties, new provisions, and new consequences, but such a newly formed covenant cannot be construed *as* the previous covenant or as *fulfillment* of that previous covenant. Figure 5 illustrates what God indicates (again see Gal. 3:17) that He will not do in reference to the covenants of Scripture.

FIGURE 5—AN ILLEGITIMATE TRANSFER OF COVENANT

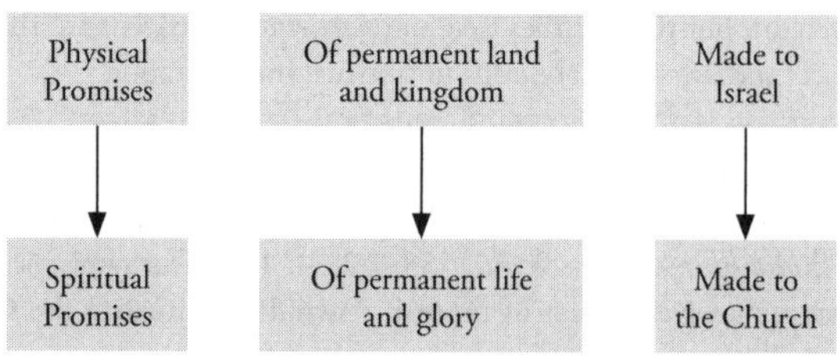

Spiritual interpretation also confuses the covenants by mixing the parties to the covenants with the provisions of the covenants. Israel's sin against Christ in rejecting and crucifying Him destroyed individual participation in the *provisions* of the covenant for those who sinned, but it did not change the *original parties*, the unilateral nature, or the consequences of the covenants. For example, in the Abrahamic Covenant, God will bless all the nations spiritually in Abraham (Gen. 12:3). God and Abraham are parties to the covenant. In this particular expression of the Abrahamic Covenant, universal blessing is the provision.

Cox asserts, "God made two sets of promises to national Israel—national promises, and spiritual promises. All earthly promises to Israel have been either fulfilled or invalidated because of disobedience. All spiritual promises are being fulfilled through the church." By this claim Cox creatively substitutes a provision of the covenant (the salvation of the Gentiles) for a party to the covenant (Abraham).[43] He treats the provisions as interchangeable and revocable in spite of the fact that God made the covenant with Abraham. This hermeneutic is badly flawed. Table 22 outlines the parties, provisions, and conditions for the Abrahamic, Davidic, and New covenants. Notice in particular that God specifically repudiates conditionality in these covenants. He vows to fulfill them exactly as He has indicated.

Table 22—A Comparison of Three OT Covenants

	Abrahamic	**Davidic**	**New**
Passage(s)	Genesis 12:1–3, 7 Genesis 13:14–17 Genesis 15:1–21 Genesis 17:1–8	2 Samuel 7:8–29	Jeremiah 31:31–40
Parties	God & Abraham	God & David	God & the house of Israel, the house of Judah
Type of Covenant	Possibly bilateral in 12:1–3 Unilateral in 12:7 and chs. 13, 15, 17	Unilateral	Unilateral

[43] Cox, 46.

	Abrahamic	Davidic	New
Provisions	Make A. a great nation (large number of descendants) Bless A. Make A.'s name great Make A. a blessing Bless those who bless A. Curse those who curse A. Bless all families of earth in A. Inheritance of the land forever as an everlasting possession Promise to extend the covenant to A.'s descendants forever	Make D. a great name Give Israel permanent security in the land Give D. rest from enemies Make a house for D. Son of D. to build temple Son will be disciplined but never cut off House, kingdom, and throne of D. will endure forever	Put My law in them, on their heart I will be their God, they will be My people All will know Me I will forgive their sin Israel will be a nation forever Jerusalem will be rebuilt Jerusalem will never be overthrown forever
Conditions	Go from country and father's house Otherwise unconditional	None	None; God specifically says nothing, not even Israel's sin, can mitigate this covenant. He will never cast off Israel.
Consequences	An individual can sever himself from the promised extension of the covenant by his own act of rebellion (Gen. 17:14).	Discipline only, no revocation possible	None stated

As we study the church in the New Testament, we observe that three of the seven provisions of the New Covenant seem to apply to the church. God sets His law in the hearts of believers; He makes them His people; and He forgives their sin. Doesn't this make the church equal spiritual Israel? No, there is no *replacement* of Israel by the church but rather an extension of some of the promises to Israel. While the *extension* of the covenant to an unforeseen (mystery) party does no violence to the original covenant, the *substitution* of new parties for old parties violates the terms of the covenant, particularly when the New Covenant specifically indicates that no distinction exists between an elusive spiritual Israel and a merely physical Israel. Spiritual Israel would imply those who are obedient to God's law, but the New Covenant indicates (1) that God will not cut off His people even for their sin and (2) that God will take non-spiritual Israel and make her spiritual by bringing her to repentance.

The second problem in understanding covenants centers on the shift from conditionality to unconditionality. A bilateral covenant possesses a sequence of responsibility. If the first party meets his requirements, the second party must fulfill his responsibilities as well. Once the first party has met his obligations, any sense of "conditionality" felt by the second party becomes unconditional. Remember the illustration of the house painting above. If I paint my friend's house within the allotted time, he must pay me the agreed-upon price. Once I have completed my obligations, no condition remains before he must pay up. Imbedded within the original terms is a contingency that can become non-contingency. Even if the original Abrahamic Covenant was bilateral, Abraham immediately believed and obeyed (Gen. 12:4). From this point onward, covenant responsibility rested entirely with God. Figure 6 expands and develops a section of figure 4. It illustrates how the sense of conditionality experienced by the second party disappears once the first party fulfills his obligations.

FIGURE 6—ORDER OF OBLIGATIONS IN A BILATERAL COVENANT

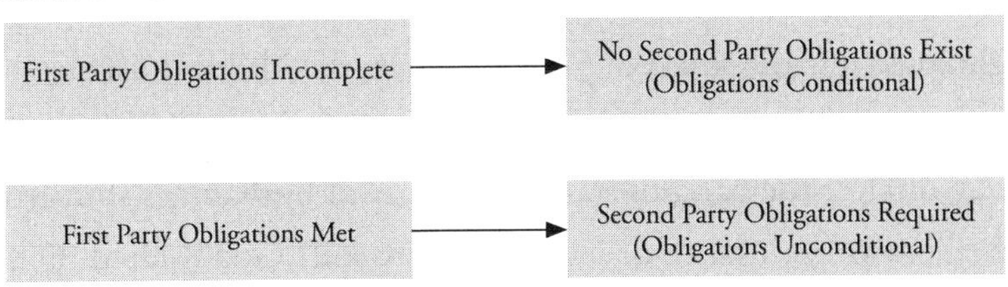

Spiritual interpretation creates a third problem by adding conditions to the original covenants. It sees conditions where the text does not cite any conditions. Why? Because the figurative system *requires* conditionality in order for it to dismiss the literal fulfillment of the promises to Israel. Adding conditions serves as a convenient solution to a problem produced by the figurative hermeneutic. There were no qualifications such as "If all (or at least the vast majority) of your descendants and the people of Israel believe in me, then I will fulfill my promises" as part of these covenants. God guaranteed His covenant fulfillment to Abraham and David.

The strongest single argument against the unconditionality of biblical covenants comes from passages such as Ezekiel 33:10–16 and Jeremiah 18:7–10 that seem to imply that God's promises come with inherent conditions even if He does not actually state those conditions.[44] Several problems attend this claim. General statements in the course of Scripture do not have the solemnity and specified provisions, parties, and consequences that covenants have. Most cultures understand the substantial difference between "I'll see you at basketball practice later today" and "With this ring I thee wed, and all my worldly goods I thee endow; in sickness and in health, in poverty or in riches, until death do us part." The former is a statement of intent that has imbedded contingencies. The latter is a vow, a strict and formal covenant. Many statements of Scripture are statements of divine intent, not of absolute promise. Just as a parent might tell a child, "We're planning to go apple picking this weekend," God reveals His intentions concerning the righteous and the wicked. Poor weather, the child's misbehavior, mechanical difficulties with the car, or work responsibilities could delay or alter the parent's stated intent. And humanity's shift from rebellion to repentance or vice versa may shift God's stated intent. Moreover, God does reveal the conditions and contingencies that

[44] See also footnote 42 above, which examines Jeremiah 18.

attend His general statements of intent. This is precisely the point of Jeremiah 18 and Ezekiel 33. God communicates much of His Word in a fashion intended to keep people from misconstruing its meaning. He knows that individuals will assume that they have lived righteously long enough and that a few "wild oats" won't hurt anything; so He reveals His will on the matter. He also knows that some people will look at their sin, feel that it is insurmountably evil, and fail to recognize that salvation is from the Lord; so He reveals His will on this matter as well. Nothing in Jeremiah 18 or Ezekiel 33 warrants the belief that God would handle His oaths in a similar fashion. What He has vowed, He will perform, not because the recipient of His promise is so wonderful, but because God is a covenant-keeping God.

The reader might balk at the gratuitous freedom that the Scriptures seem to grant to the recipients of the covenants. It seems that Israel can do no wrong as far as the covenants are concerned, even while she does much wrong as far as personal conduct is concerned. If we substitute *grace* for *gratuitous* and *election* for *freedom*, however, Israel's condition seems not so unlike that of believers in Christ, who insist (rightly) that their condition in Christ is secure in spite of their sin.[45] Yet many theologians who defend the unconditional election of the church are quick to deny the unconditional election of Israel. The spiritualization of the Old Testament covenants is theologically schizophrenic. The addition of conditionality to God's oaths is theologically inconsistent.

[45] Ironically, those who trumpet the security of believers in Christ most loudly often deny that God could operate on the same "gracious election + sovereign guarantee" pattern with reference to Israel. Their defense of the security of believers is absolutely correct, and their denial of Israel's national restoration is absolutely wrong.

An illustration might help.[46] Suppose I had ten students in a New Testament Introduction class. As we approached a particular test, I promised the students that anyone who earned an "A" on that test would receive three benefits: (1) an in-class ice cream party, (2) coffee supplied by the teacher for the remainder of the semester, and (3) an automatic "A" in the entire New Testament Introduction course overall. Suppose that three students earned an "A" on the test and seven did not. Would I be faithful and true to my word if I revoked the promise to those who earned the "A"? Certainly not. What if I went ahead with my promise as originally given, and on the day of the ice cream party ten students showed up from my Problems of Interpretation class and received ice cream alongside the New Testament Introduction students? Have I violated the first promise by including members of another class in certain provisions originally offered to a different class? Not unless I shifted the promises to the second class away from the first. Can I give all of the provisions to the members of the second class? No, since the Problems of Interpretation students are not enrolled in New Testament Introduction, I cannot give them an "A" in New Testament Introduction. Figure 7 below illustrates this distribution of covenant blessings.

---

[46] I am indebted to Dr. Layton Talbert for this illustration. While I have tweaked some of the details, the thought is his.

FIGURE 7—THE DISTRIBUTION OF COVENANT BLESSINGS

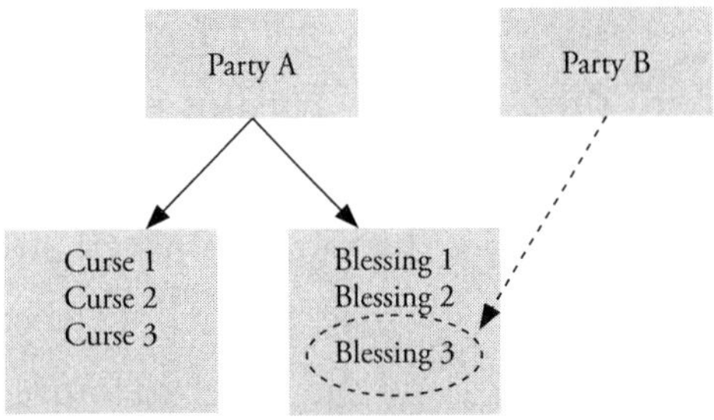

Such are the promises of Scripture. God made covenants with Abraham, David, and the house of Israel/Jacob (Party A above) that He will not revoke or revise. He can extend some of the blessings of these covenants to additional parties (the church, Party B above) as He sees fit. This makes the second party a sharer in some of the provisions of the covenant made with the first party without revoking the provision for the first party. He may not extend all of the promises to the new parties (land promise, Blessings 1–2 above). When the interpreter comes to the New Testament and sees some of the blessings of the New Covenant applied to the church, he might assume that God has "spiritualized" the covenant and removed Israel's national participation in it, but he would be mistaken. God will not go back on His promises. Romans 11:1–32 indicates exactly the situation above. The spiritual interpretation does violence to the covenants of Scripture when it recognizes correctly that the church experiences some of the blessings of the covenants but turns this recognition into a usurping of those covenants from Israel.

Select Additional Statements of Biblical Covenants

How can the reader possibly construe the following statements as either bilateral (conditional) or figurative?

> In a little wrath I hid my face from thee for a moment; but with everlasting kindness will I have mercy on thee, saith the Lord thy Redeemer. For this is as the waters of Noah unto me: for as I have sworn that the waters of Noah should no more go over the earth; so have I sworn that I would not be wroth with thee, nor rebuke thee. For the mountains shall depart, and the hills be removed; but my kindness shall not depart from thee, neither shall the covenant of my peace be removed, saith the Lord that hath mercy on thee (Isa. 54:8–10).

Context will not allow a spiritual application of the passage to the church (1) since the same national Israel that receives God's judgment in the preceding context receives this promise and (2) since verse 3 indicates that Israel would inherit the cities of the Gentiles. Moreover, God's covenant with national Israel is as sure as His covenant with Noah that He would never again destroy the entire earth with a flood! If one spiritualizes the promise to Israel, he must spiritualize the promise to Noah, since the Noahic Covenant serves as the point of comparison. God will not revoke His covenants.

> And now therefore thus saith the Lord, the God of Israel, concerning this city, whereof ye say, It shall be delivered into the hand of the king of Babylon by the sword, and by the famine, and by the pestilence; behold, I will gather them out of all countries, whither I have driven them in mine anger, and in my fury, and in great wrath; and I will bring them again unto this place, and I will cause them to dwell safely: and they shall be my people, and I will be their God: and I will give them one heart, and one way, that they may fear me for ever, for the good of them, and

> of their children after them: and I will make an everlasting covenant with them, that I will not turn away from them, to do them good; but I will put my fear in their hearts, that they shall not depart from me. Yea, I will rejoice over them to do them good, and I will plant them in this land assuredly with my whole heart and with my whole soul. For thus saith the Lord; Like as I have brought all this great evil upon this people, so will I bring upon them all the good that I have promised them (Jer. 32:36–42).

The very city, Jerusalem, that was overthrown by Babylon would be rebuilt and restored, and just as God wrecked Israel, He promises to bring Israel to repentance. He vows to do so not because of their righteousness, their obedience, or their seeking after Him. He promises to draw them by His own sovereign power and will:

> Thus saith the Lord; If ye can break my covenant of the day, and my covenant of the night, and that there should not be day and night in their season; then may also my covenant be broken with David my servant, that he should not have a son to reign upon his throne; and with the Levites the priests, my ministers. As the host of heaven cannot be numbered, neither the sand of the sea measured: so will I multiply the seed of David my servant, and the Levites that minister unto me (Jer. 33:20–22).

Notice carefully what the passage indicates. It does not say that if day and night ever cease, then the covenant could be broken. It says that if you can break the covenant of day and night, then a possibility would exist for the Davidic and Levitical covenants to be broken. There is no possibility of the former; so there is no possibility of the latter. David's throne must be established on earth in Jerusalem according to God's promise, and the Levites must be restored to a special place of ministry or the language of Scripture and the promises of God have no discernible meaning whatsoever.

Figurative interpretation has a significant burden of proof to meet, and it cannot meet that burden without utterly destroying the intelligibility of Scripture. We simply cannot make questionable what God has vowed is irrevocable, and we cannot make conditional what God has called unconditional. The prophetic passages cited above do not abound with imaginative details or symbolic representations. They are straightforwardly literal. Therefore, as a method of interpretation, the symbolic method does great violence to the counsel of Scripture.

Representative Defects in Interpretation[47]

So far we have treated systemic problems with the symbolic method. Now we will turn to specific instances of exegetical weakness.

Matthew 21:18–19

Symbolic interpreters believe that Matthew 21:18–19 indicates the loss of covenant promises for Israel.

> Now in the morning as he returned into the city, he hungered. And when he saw a fig tree in the way, he came to it, and found nothing thereon, but leaves only, and said unto

[47] The passages chosen in this section stem directly from major works that are defending the symbolic interpretation of prophecy. These include but are not limited to Allis's *Prophecy and the Church*, Cox's *Amillennialism Today*, and Benjamin Merkle's "Old Testament Restoration Prophecies Regarding the Nation of Israel: Literal or Symbolic?" *Southern Baptist Theological Journal* 14, no. 1 (Spring 2010): 14–25. In other words, I have not fabricated a series of easy passages to refute. These are the types of passages that spiritual interpreters use to warrant their revoking of the covenants with Israel.

> it, Let no fruit grow on thee henceforward for ever. And presently the fig tree withered away.

In order to make this interpretation work, the reader must spiritualize the text.[48] The fig tree must equal Israel, the cursing of that fig tree must mean the destruction of Jerusalem, and its barrenness must indicate the revocation of God's covenant promises to Israel. After he allegorizes his data in this location, he uses this dubious interpretation to justify his spiritualizing elsewhere in Scripture. This permits his reduction and spiritualization of the covenants and promises given to Israel in the Old Testament.

In the immediate context, the disciples' response to Jesus' cursing the fig tree has nothing to do with a revocation of the covenant with Israel. Christ used the lesson to teach the disciples about faith and prayer, not about the loss of a covenant. The context shows us Christ's meaning, and the symbolic interpreter's reading of the passage does not match the divinely ordained interpretation. The figurative method allegorizes the passage inappropriately in order to justify allegorizing other passages.

Matthew 21:42–45

The assumption that Matthew 21:42–45 revokes God's covenant promises to Israel and grants those promises to the church also lacks textual warrant.

> Jesus saith unto them, Did ye never read in the scriptures, The stone which the builders rejected, the same is become the head of the corner: this is the Lord's doing, and it is marvellous in our eyes? Therefore say I unto you, The

[48] "The Jewish state came to a bitter end in A.D. 70. Nor will national Israel ever again be a fruitful nation. This fact is made obvious by Jesus' curse on the fig tree" (Cox, 43).

> kingdom of God shall be taken from you, and given to a nation bringing forth the fruits thereof. And whosoever shall fall on this stone shall be broken: but on whomsoever it shall fall, it will grind him to powder. And when the chief priests and Pharisees had heard his parables, they perceived that he spake of them.

Symbolic interpreters force their own ideas upon this passage. First, the reader must turn *nation* into the church. This is a creative expedient but one that lacks justification in this passage. Second, the prophets expected Israel's repeated rebellion. They frequently indicated that judgment followed Israel's sin, but these same men prophesied in the same immediate contexts that one day God would work graciously to bring about national Israel's repentance and restoration.[49] They expected a coming, obedient, national Israel, created by God's power (see figure 8 below).

Third, interpreting Matthew 21:42–45 in a symbolic fashion destroys the consistency of the Old Testament prophecies. Israel's judgment and restoration are parallel. Figure 8 illustrates this. The only box in question in the figure is the box that concerns the promises of blessing and restoration. Symbolic interpretation applies these to the church. This is a hermeneutical fallacy. If the threat to a national group of people was fulfilled literally, then the blessing to the same group of people must also be fulfilled literally. No textual warrant exists for the manipulation of the term *Israel* so

---

[49] "Indeed, there arise a number of points in Scripture in which prophecies of judgment, literally fulfilled, are balanced contextually by prophecies of restoration, that would seem to necessitate a correspondingly literal fulfillment." J. Barton Payne, *The Theology of the Older Testament* (Grand Rapids: Zondervan, 1962), 491.

that it has two radically different referents in the same immediate context.[50]

FIGURE 8—THE PATTERN OF THE OT PROPHECIES REGARDING ISRAEL

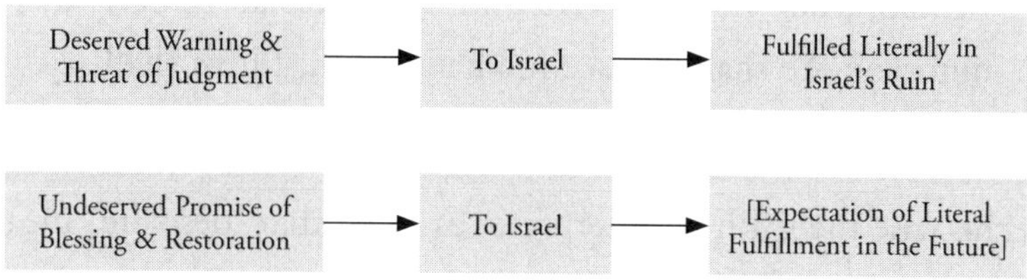

Fourth, and crucially determinative, a figurative interpretation ignores the fact that Jesus was addressing the "chief priests and the elders of the people" (v. 23). It is "they" who were conspiring against Jesus (vv. 23, 25–27), and it was "to them" (vv. 31, 42) that Jesus issued His parable, challenge, and warning. Those who should have been in the vanguard accepting Jesus were rejecting Him instead. They would lose their place in the blessing that God has guaranteed to Israel, but no revocation of the national promise appears in this passage. Paying attention to the biblical context solves the "problem" imagined by symbolic interpreters. True, the elders represented the people in some ways, but it was never true that all the people of Israel rejected Messiah. Believing Jews have always existed so that even if God's covenant with Israel were conditional (and the Old Testament says it is not), He must keep His covenant with those who believe in and obey Him.

[50] Symbolic interpreters charge Dispensationalism with granting Israel a "blank check" to do whatever she wants. Dispensationalists reply: (1) God, not we, granted Israel the certainty of restoration; (2) the Old Testament contexts do not indicate that any and every Jew will receive the blessing, but that (3) God will work sovereignly in Israel's behalf in much the same way that He works to draw any man to salvation; and (4) that sovereign work will result in the national repentance of Israel in the future, which in turn will result in Israel's receiving the blessing as promised.

Matthew 23:38–39

In Matthew 23:38–39, we finally meet a passage that has at least some bearing on national Israel:

> Behold, your house is left unto you desolate. For I say unto you, Ye shall not see me henceforth, till ye shall say, Blessed is he that cometh in the name of the Lord.

In this case the spiritual interpreter assumes that "desolate" means the revocation of all physical promises to national Israel, and then he omits verse 39, which concerns the restoration of the same national, racial group. In other words, although Jesus clearly indicates the ruin of that immediate generation of national Jews, He does not revoke the promises given to Israel in the Old Testament, nor does He spiritualize any prophecy. One day Israel will repent. It will accept Christ as Messiah. It will call out, "Blessed is He who comes in the name of the Lord." This passage simply does not warrant the symbolic interpretive method.

Romans 9:24–26

Many interpreters use Romans 9:24–26 as proof that the New Testament spiritualizes Old Testament prophecies concerning Israel, but closer examination reveals significant problems with this assessment.[51] Specifically, symbolic interpreters believe that Paul's citation of Hosea makes the church the fulfillment of the Old Testament prophecy.

> I will call them my people, which were not my people; and her beloved, which was not beloved. And it shall come to pass, that in the place where it was said unto them, Ye are

[51] Not only amillennialists, but even some historic premillennialists misinterpret this important passage. See, for example, George Eldon Ladd, "Historic Premillennialism," in *The Meaning of the Millennium*, 23–24.

> not my people; there shall they be called the children of the living God (Rom. 9:25–26, citing Hosea 1:10; 2:23).

Romans 9 does mention Gentiles once in the near context (v. 24), and Paul does quote the Old Testament passage, but calling Gentile salvation the "fulfillment" of Hosea is a misinterpretation of Paul's point. First, the context of verses 25–26 indicates that Paul is using a logical-argumentative pattern to demonstrate that God elects sovereignly and unconditionally. The point is not the direct application of any prophecy to the Gentiles. Second, Paul never uses the *fulfillment* terminology of the Hosea passage. Instead, the passage uses Hosea as an *illustration* of the truth that God elects a "not my people" to be "my people." That God has done this repeatedly through history—prior to Israel in the patriarchs, later in reference to Israel, and now in the church—makes Him a consistent God, but that He has done so repeatedly does not mean that His first election equals the second. Suppose my son were to say, "Daddy, I'm afraid I won't get any birthday presents," and I replied, "Buddy, don't worry. You saw Daddy give your sister presents just three weeks ago." Should he interpret my response to mean that he would receive her presents? No, I was comforting him by illustrating my character. He should infer that a dad who operates on this pattern has planned for his well-being. Romans 9:25–26 simply will not bear the weight of interpretation that the spiritual method lays on it.

Matthew 2:15

Matthew 2:15 cites Hosea 11:1 in an unusual fashion. Hosea says, "When Israel was a child, then I loved him, and called my son out of Egypt." Matthew comments on the early days of Jesus' life with "that it might be fulfilled which was spoken of the Lord by the prophet, saying, Out of Egypt have I called my son." At first glance

Matthew's adaptation seems to spiritualize Old Testament prophecy, but this is not the best assessment of Matthew's intent. First, Hosea was not engaged in predictive prophecy in 11:1. Thus, at very least, Matthew's use of Hosea does not warrant the wholesale spiritualization of predictive prophecy concerning Israel and Judah. Hosea looks backward at the historic Exodus event. Matthew looks backward to the Exodus as well, using the wording of Hosea to express the undeniable reality that Jesus Christ is the Son of God in a unique way. Since Hosea was not predictive, Matthew's term *fulfillment* can hardly mean "carrying out a predicted event." Rather he indicates that Jesus Christ is the Son of God, Who identified with Israel not as Israel's replacement but as the promised seed, the One to Whom all the prophets point.[52] Second, nothing in the context warrants figurative interpretation at all. *Egypt* means "Egypt." *Son* means "son." *Out of* means "out of." It is disturbing to see spiritual interpreters take such a passage as justifying the type of hermeneutical shift that makes Israel equal the church, land promises equal spiritual blessings, and Davidic monarchy equal a heavenly reign, especially when such interpreters are not under direct inspiration of the Holy Spirit in their handling of the Old Testament.

Hebrews 8

Hebrews demonstrates Christ's superiority to the prophets, to angels, and to the Levitical priests. In the attempt to magnify Christ's offices, some interpreters have pressed certain passages in Hebrews beyond their meaning. Strained exegesis may seem to produce a

---

[52] In discussing this very interplay between Hosea 11:1 and Matthew 2:14–15, Henry A. Virkler and Karelynne Gerber Ayayo note, "When the fulfillment passages are typological, the New Testament writers present the typology not as the *meaning* of the Old Testament text but as a contemporary event analogous to God's past actions" (italics mine). *Hermeneutics: Principles and Processes of Biblical Interpretation* (Grand Rapids: Baker Academic, 2007), 50.

nobler and more Christ-honoring meaning, but it actually degrades Christ's person by reducing His office to one time and place when it actually encompasses far more. In particular, Hebrews 8 couples Jeremiah's New Covenant with the covenant granted by Jesus Christ. The argument seems airtight. If Jesus administers the New Covenant through His blood, and the church receives the New Covenant, then Israel forfeited the New Covenant. This extrapolates far beyond what one should reasonably infer from the text. It also falls prey to strained logic. Christ can extend some of the promises of the New Covenant to a mystery body (the church, unforeseen in the Old Testament) without replacing Israel with the church, without equating Israel with the church, and without applying all of the New Covenant promises to the church. Hebrews 8 teaches that the church shares in the spiritual aspects of the New Covenant (see figure 4 above). In addition, the Old Covenant spoken of in Hebrews 8 is the Mosaic law, not the Abrahamic or Davidic covenants.[53] Hebrews 8 simply does not warrant the spiritualization of Old Testament prophecies.

Restoration Reiterated

The Old Testament foresees that God would cut off Israel from the land for a time and would cast off His temple but never indicates that He would "cut off" His people in any absolute sense (1 Kings 9:7). The individual participation of later Israelites in the land promise might have been conditional (Deut. 29:28), but the land promise itself was not conditional. Interestingly, Jeremiah 31:35–40 guarantees to the seed of Israel (not the seed of Abraham) the

---

[53] Paying attention to the context keeps us from comparing the wrong covenants. The immediately preceding verses reference the law and the priesthood of Israel, neither of which were components of the Abrahamic or Davidic covenants. The New Covenant replaces the Mosaic Covenant. It apparently does not replace the Abrahamic or Davidic covenants.

fulfillment of New Covenant promises. In fact, just two chapters later in Jeremiah 33:23–26, God specifically says that although unbelieving people *say* Israel is cast off forever, God will never cast off Israel forever. He repudiates this as falsehood. The assertion that God has cut off Israel is flawed in that it directly contradicts God's emphatic declaration. His covenant is fixed regardless of what Israel does. Ezekiel 11:16–21 anticipates God's regathering His people. He vows to make them holy forever. Zechariah 10:6 indicates that God will recall those whom He has cast off for a season.

God knows Israel's sin. He never excuses it. He promises to judge it severely, but He guarantees that no sin will ever void His covenant with the nation of Israel (Hosea 14:4–7; Joel 2:18–27; 3:16–21; Amos 9:8–15; Mic. 7:18–20; Zeph. 3:13–20; Zech. 12:14). Spiritualizing Old Testament prophecies in order to see their fulfillment in the church is not a noble or well-directed enterprise.

Spiritualization in Christ's First Advent

Many spiritual interpreters use the life of Christ to justify their spiritualization of Old Testament prophecy.[54] Putting their argument into a syllogistic form in figure 9 below helps us analyze the thought process. In the following lines *P* stands for a premise and *C* for a conclusion. Following rules of logic, once a conclusion has been reached, it becomes a premise in the sustained argument.

[54] Benjamin L. Merkle, for example, lists "the central role of Jesus' death and resurrection in salvation history" among his reasons for interpreting symbolically ("Old Testament Restoration Prophecies," 15). His other reasons include "the true nature of biblical religion" (which is simply a false dichotomy), "the unique genre of biblical prophecy" (which is circular reasoning since it assumes what it is trying to prove), and "the symbolic manner in which the New Testament interprets Old Testament prophecies" (which I have addressed in the specific passages above). Merkle fixates on the need for the Old Testament prophecies to be "intelligible" to their immediate audience, but intelligibility at the expense of accuracy is worthless. In this case the Jews correctly understood fictional promises and events.

FIGURE 9—LOGICAL ARGUMENT FOR SPIRITUALIZING PROPHECY

P^1—Christ is God's ultimate revelation in time and space.	T
P^2—Christ has already come.	T
C^1/P^3—God's ultimate revelation has already come in time and space.	T
P^4—Much Old Testament prophecy did not occur literally when Christ came.	T
P^5—God cannot lie.	T
C^2/P^6—OT prophecies must apply spiritually, not literally, to Christ.	F
C^3/P^7—We must interpret all OT prophecy through the lens of Christ's first advent.	F
C^4—A predominantly literal hermeneutic is false.	F

All conservative interpreters should be able to agree with the first five premises, but the literal interpreter observes that C^2 does not follow from P^1–P^5. The spiritual interpretation of prophecy has several unstated underlying premises. In order for C^2 to follow logically from the preceding argument, an additional premise (P^A) must exist: Christ had to have fulfilled in His first advent (nearly) all that the Old Testament expected the Messiah to do. When P^A is added, the syllogism becomes valid, but not true. P^A is false, resulting in a false conclusion (C^2) followed by a series of additional false conclusions (C^3, C^4). To say that Christ is the *fulfillment* of Old Testament expectations, covenants, and promises does not equal the claim that Christ *has fulfilled* all Old Testament expectations, covenants, and promises. Christ is the fulfillment because He will bring to pass every promise of God. Nothing in Scripture requires that every Old Testament prophecy had to be fulfilled in His first advent. In fact, every orthodox system admits as much by acknowledging the Second Coming. How, then, can the insertion of the flawed premise (P^A) occur? Because a chosen ecclesiology (Israel = the church) overrides interpretive controls. P^A is demonstrably false, but it is tacitly necessary in order to justify the equation of Israel and the church as well as the symbolic interpretation of prophecy.

Inaugurating a promise and fulfilling that promise may not occur simultaneously. For instance, assuming that the Spirit's descent at Pentecost must fulfill all of Joel's prophecy at that time (Acts 2:17–21) overreaches proper biblical interpretation. We know without doubt that Jesus fulfilled portions of the Prophets in His first advent while reserving other portions for His Second Coming (Luke 4:18–19 citing Isa. 61). Inauguration does not equal final and complete fulfillment. Many interpreters confuse this point and demand a first-advent fulfillment for national, physical promises to Israel. Finding none, they resort to spiritualizing those promises when a better alternative exists: Christ will yet fulfill all remaining Old Testament prophecies at His Second Coming.

Conclusion

This appendix has examined the arguments for a symbolic interpretation of prophecy in general and of Revelation in particular. It has argued that an adequate warrant does not exist for the hermeneutical shift from a literal to a symbolic method in interpretation. The decision concerning an interpretive method determines the outcome of interpretation. A symbolic method will likely yield a preterist, historicist, or idealist interpretation and a corresponding adherence to Postmillennialism or Amillennialism. The roads of interpretation really do diverge radically at this point. A refutation of some of the primary arguments used by symbolic interpreters to build a case for their method does not prove that symbolism is absent from Revelation. It does, however, indicate that a predominantly symbolic interpretation of prophecy has not proved its case sufficiently to overturn a normal, literal method of interpretation.

Appendix 2:
An Interpretive Survey of Symbols

Revelation utilizes symbols.[1] You should not construe this statement as contradicting the tenor and argument of this book. Like any other work of literature, Revelation uses many figures of speech, including symbols. This section discusses the known symbols that exist in Revelation and documents their interpretations where possible. Once the reader has charted the boundaries of the known and the unknown, he can often figure out at least portions of the unknown. To begin with, we will use table 23 to note the undisputed symbols by chapter in Revelation.[2]

Table 23—Symbols in Revelation & Their Interpretations

Symbol		Interpretation	
Seven candlesticks	1:12–13; 2:1, 5	Seven churches	1:20
Seven stars	1:16	Seven angels	1:20
Sword	1:16; 2:12, 16; 19:15, 21	Word of God	Heb. 4:12
Key	1:18; 3:7; 9:1; 20:1	Authority	Isa. 22:22; Matt. 16:19
Bed	2:22	Tribulation	2:22
Garments	3:4, 18	Deeds of the saints	19:8
Opened door	3:8	Exercise of authority	Isa. 22:22

[1] See "Treating Figures of Speech in Revelation" in chapter 1.

[2] We must remember that the fact that we have no personal experience with an entity does not necessarily make it symbolic. The table treats only undisputed symbols, not every metaphor in the book. For example, some interpreters see the "seven Spirits" (1:4), "the first-born" (1:5), and the "clouds" (1:7) as symbols; but since 5:6 uses a symbol for the seven spirits, the "firstborn" is a title rather than a symbol, and the clouds are just as likely entirely literal, they will not appear in the list. Table 23 includes metonymy in the category of symbols. Metonymy replaces a word with another word that is closely associated with it. In the phrase "key of David" the word *key* stands for "authority."

Symbol		Interpretation	
Pillar	3:12	Secure believer Gal. 2:9; or household of God 1 Tim. 3:15	
Gold	3:18	Meaningful works	1 Cor. 3:12
Seven lamps of fire	4:5	Seven spirits of God	4:5
Lion of Judah	5:5	Powerful ruler	Num. 24:9; Mic. 5:8
Root of David	5:5	Davidic heir and king	Isa. 11:1
Lamb	5:6	Sacrifice for the people	Too numerous to cite
Seven horns	5:6	Power	Deut. 33:17; 2 Sam. 22:3
Seven eyes	5:6	Seven spirits of God	5:6
A star fallen	9:1	Spiritual creature	cf. 1:20
Two olive trees Two candlesticks	11:4	Two witnesses	11:3
The great city Sodom and Egypt	11:8	Where the Lord was crucified	11:8
Woman clothed with sun wilderness, place prepared, two wings of an eagle, earth drank the flood, rest of her offspring	12:1ff.	No interpretation given[3]	
A great red dragon seven heads, ten horns, seven crowns, third of the stars of heaven, water like a river (cf. 17:3)	12:3, 4, 15	Serpent of old, devil, Satan	12:9
Beast coming from the sea ten horns, seven heads, ten diadems (cf. 17:3)	13:1	Antichrist	Dan. 7:23; 11:36ff. Rev. 17:8
Another beast horns like a lamb	13:11	A false prophet	13:13–14
666	13:18	Number of the beast	13:18
Wine	14:10	Wrath of God	14:10; 19:15
Sickle	14:14, 16	"Reaping" people	14:16, 18
Great harlot riding the red beast, clothed in purple and red, adorned with gold and precious stones	17:1; 19:2	Babylon	17:5

[3] Significantly, where Scripture provides no clear interpretation, it explicitly indicates that an image is a symbol lest it be mistaken for a literal event.

Symbol		Interpretation	
Seven heads	17:3	Seven mountains, that is, seven kings	17:9–10
Ten horns	17:3	Ten kings reigning with the beast	17:12
Wine	18:3	Immorality	18:3
Bride, wife of the Lamb	21:9	New Jerusalem, holy city	21:10
Dogs	22:15	Evildoers	Phil. 3:2

Although many interpreters inflate this list to include virtually every image in Revelation, these are the symbols that most interpreters agree on. Several conclusions stem from such a chart. First, where interpreters agree on the presence of a symbol, they do so because Scripture explicitly interprets the symbol. Revelation does use symbolism, but in the vast majority of instances it tells us what the symbol means.

Second, in the most highly symbolic section of the entire book (chs. 12–13), Revelation indicates twice that the visions in the section are symbolic (12:1, 3). If God intended for us to interpret the entire book symbolically, why does He explicitly indicate that these localized visions were symbols? It seems more natural to accept the book as predominantly literal. Where Revelation departs from the normal, Scripture-wide hermeneutic, it explicitly indicates the departure so that the reader will not misunderstand what it is revealing.

Third, there are not nearly as many symbols as the reader might first assume. Revelation has over 9,800 words in its Greek text spread over its twenty-two chapters, and yet it has somewhere between thirty and fifty symbols, virtually all of which have a direct explanation in the text. Pastors and teachers have shied away from this book for too long, assuming that its esoteric symbolism puts the book out of most believers' reach. But God did not give us Revelation as an appendix to Scripture. It bears a revelatory intent, doctrinal instruction, and practical application like that of the other biblical books, and we ought to be preaching and teaching it in a balanced fashion in the church.

Fourth, the fact that we do not have personal experience with the types of things that occur in Revelation does not mean that the events are symbolic or mythical. Some kind of supernatural locust-creatures do exist (ch. 9). We have never seen them. We can hardly conjure up a picture of them in our own minds, but we can accept the fact that there are parts of the spirit world that we do not understand. Turning such images into symbols without adequate warrant blunts the force of Scripture. It also expresses an overweening confidence in one's knowledge of all that is and could possibly be. According to Scripture many thrones, dominions, principalities, powers, and rulers exist in the spirit world (Rom. 8:38; Eph. 3:10; 6:12; Col. 1:16). Scripture does not call on us to learn them, to manipulate them, or to fear them, but Revelation briefly pulls back the curtain on their existence and actions.

What does this survey of symbols mean for us? It seems to add credibility to the assertion that God communicated this book in a manner intended for our understanding. Where symbols exist, they either have a contextual interpretation, a broader biblical interpretation, or a clear enough referent for the interpreter to grasp what is happening.